The

—

Better

—

Part

Thomas Keating

The
Better
Part

Stages of
Contemplative Living

Continuum
New York · London

2000
The Continuum International Publishing Group Inc
370 Lexington Avenue, New York, NY 10017

The Continuum International Publishing Group Ltd
Wellington House, 125 Strand, London WC2R 0BB

Printed in the United States of America

Library of Congress Cataloging-in-Publication Data

Keating, Thomas.
The better part : stages of the contemplative life / by Thomas Keating.
p. cm.
ISBN 0-8245-1229-7
1. Contemplation – Congresses. 2. Spiritual life – Catholic Church –
Congresses. I. Title.

BV5091.C7 K413 2000
248.3′4 – dc21

99-087072

To
Father Laurence Freeman
and
The World Community of Christian Meditation

CONTENTS

ACKNOWLEDGMENTS ·

Thanks to Bonnie J. Shimizu and Robert Dunbar
for their editorial help.

FOREWORD

READING THIS BOOK has recalled for me the happy sunlit days of the 1998 John Main Seminar led by Father Thomas Keating in San Francisco. It increases the happiness of those memories to know that his teaching, which so delighted the participants at the seminar, is now being shared with a far wider audience.

I first met Father Thomas twenty-one years before this seminar when, as a young monk, not yet fully professed, I had just arrived with John Main in North America to establish a Benedictine community committed to the teaching and practice of meditation in the Christian tradition. I visited the then Abbot Thomas at St. Joseph's Abbey in Spencer, Massachusetts, and told him of our work and vision and heard in turn of his work in the teaching of Centering Prayer. I was struck by his attentiveness and unselfish interest in our experience. I left feeling encouraged by the sense of a shared vision and that the subtle differences in the two schools of prayer were in no way divisions but signs of the richness of the Christian contemplative spirit. This I shared with Father

John, who sadly was never to meet Father Thomas in person but whose work he respected and admired.

The John Main Seminar has been held annually in his honor since 1984 as the major international event of the World Community for Christian Meditation. Previous presenters have included Jean Vanier, Bede Griffiths, William Johnston, the Dalai Lama, and Mary McAleese. Each seminar has afforded the opportunity for a major thinker or teacher in his or her own field to reflect on important aspects of modern life in a way that highlights the spiritual and contemplative dimension. In so doing we have felt that it also assists the necessary reinstatement of this spiritual perspective into the thought, planning and practice of the modern world.

As a renowned teacher of the Christian contemplative tradition with a driving awareness of the power of prayer to change lives and the world, Father Thomas was a natural choice for presenter. His acceptance of the invitation to lead the John Main Seminar was also an opportunity to demonstrate and deepen the spiritual friendship between Contemplative Outreach and the World Community for Christian Meditation — two different but complementary expressions of the search for spiritual depth and the renewal of Christian life in our time.

Father Thomas's enlightening commentary on the contemplative meaning of the Gospel, particularly the story of the Bethany trio of Martha, Mary, and Lazarus, held his original audience in that state of alert suspense and wakeful animation that happens at a time of great spiritual enrichment. His capacity to listen to the Word of Scripture as well as to the silent depths of the contemplative experience itself is what radiates here and throughout his teaching and writing.

Some months after the seminar I was waiting for a plane connection at the Denver airport when I spotted at a distance a tall stooped figure that looked uncannily like Father Thomas. On closer examination it turned out to be no illusion but the man himself returning from a teaching weekend. We spent, in both senses, a happy hour sharing reflections on the different retreats we had just been leading. As we parted I thought of those chance meetings of the monks of the desert of the fourth century which both refreshed them and often left a word for posterity. The seminar itself had been such a meeting and the reading of this book may be the same in a different way for many more.

The Better Part fits into the great monastic tradition of Christian teaching. A monk reflects on Scripture in the light of experience. He leaves a word that startles his listeners into realizing that tradition is not a matter of theories of secondhand experience but the living and human self-transmission of Christ to his disciples. In their different ways Thomas Keating and John Main both point, through faith and experience, to this Master as well as to the depth and vigor of this tradition to help us meet the challenges of the new era on which we are now embarked.

FATHER LAURENCE FREEMAN, OSB
January 1, 2000

 **ONE**

THE HOUSEHOLD OF BETHANY

As they went on their way, he entered a village and a woman named Martha received him into her house. She had a sister called Mary who sat at the Lord's feet and listened to his teaching. But Martha was distracted with much serving and she went to him and said, "Lord, do you not care that my sister has left me to serve alone? Tell her then to help me." The Lord answered her, "Martha, Martha, you are anxious and troubled about many things. One thing is needed. Mary has chosen the better part and it shall not be taken away from her." (Luke 11:38–42)

A S WE PONDER OVER THESE WORDS, it becomes evident that the family of Bethany is a household of persons at various stages of the spiritual life.

Martha is clearly the one who best represents ourselves. She is having trouble with her false self. She is thoroughly devoted to the Lord. They are friends. Jesus loved to stop at her home. She exemplifies "good souls" at the beginning of the spiritual journey when they have the best intentions to serve God. But on this occasion Martha is upset and anxious. She is converted on the conscious level of her psychological awareness, but not converted on the unconscious level of her motivation. She is under the influence of the emotional baggage that she has carried with her from early childhood, and consisting of the three basic energy centers of the human organism.

These three basic energy centers develop out of the instinctual needs of every infant for security and survival, affection and esteem, and power and control. These are biological necessities. When they are withheld, which is everybody's experience to some degree, we either develop compensatory attitudes or repress the painful frustrations of those needs into the unconscious. There the energy remains secretly influencing our behavior and our decision-making processes.

Martha: The Purgative Way

Our first conversion focuses on trying to straighten out and clean up our ordinary conscious life. Martha is doing this. She is in the first stage of the spiritual journey — the Purgative Way. The Purgative Way consists in becoming aware of how our unconscious needs affect ordinary daily life including our service of God. It is unsettling for us to realize that, mixed in with our good intentions, are these infantile attitudes. They are necessary in early childhood in order to survive, but totally inappropriate now that we have grown up.

Martha is preparing a great dinner for Jesus. She resents his detached attitude towards her labors. She confronts him saying, "Don't you care that my sister is sitting idle at your feet? Tell her to help me." Notice the undertone of indignation. In the beginning of our spiritual journey we often have a co-dependent relationship with God. For example, we might say to God, "Give me what I want or else I won't pray any more." Although Martha is busy serving Jesus, her motivation is shot through with selfishness. The source of her frustration seems to be that she has lost control of the situation. She can't get the dinner out on time. Her sister is no help. Any time we are upset by anything, the source of the problem is primarily in ourselves. Complaining about Mary sitting at Jesus' feet is Martha's way of projecting her problem on to somebody else. Martha needs to let go of her attachment to the results of her work. She is active in the service of God but her activity is not contemplative service. She is working for herself. No doubt she thinks she is working solely for God, but in fact her motivation is mixed.

The apostles Peter, James, and John were in the same boat. They were human beings like the rest of us with all kinds of problems. Afflictive emotions like grief, anger, jealousy, envy, vanity, discouragement, and pride are rooted in the fact that we don't know what our real motivation is. The thrust of Jesus' initial teaching in the Gospel is the challenge to *grow up!* Our drive to obtain the symbols in an environment of security and survival, affection and esteem, and power and control is doomed to frustration. Martha virtually says to Jesus, "You had better get that sister of mine to help me if you want something to eat!" Jesus replies, "Martha!" We can almost feel the gentle tone of rebuke in Jesus' voice, "Martha. You are troubled about many things, but only one thing is necessary. Mary has chosen the better part and it will not be taken away from her."

That was Jesus' word of wisdom for Martha. A word of wisdom is not necessarily a rebuke. It is simply a statement of fact. There is nothing wrong with Martha's activity. It is her motivation that is defective. In Christianity, motivation is everything.

Mary: The Illuminative Way

Let us now take a look at Mary's activity, or rather, her lack of activity. She is sitting at the feet of Jesus listening to his words. Her whole attention is focused on the Master. She is listening at a level much deeper than her ears can hear. It is the kind of listening that takes place when our spiritual faculties begin to vibrate to the divine life present in Christ. One who hears the word of God on this level keeps it.

Mary is not doing anything but listening, yet as she listens her attention moves beyond the words or even the physical appearance of Jesus. She penetrates to the divine Person present in the humanity that is visible and palpable. Her faith is expanding. Listening to the words of Jesus is not so much paying attention to what is said, but rather to the experience that is communicated at the deepest level of our being by the divine presence. This is what attracts us. It is not just the words, but the eternal Word of God that we assimilate and by which we are assimilated. This is what makes us Christians — and at the same time, it makes us pray in our very *being*. This is the ultimate purpose of every form of prayer, devotion, ritual, or sacrament. The word of God in Scripture orientates us towards the transformation of our entire being. "God the Father spoke only one word and he spoke it in an eternal silence, and it is in silence that we hear it" (St. John of the Cross, *Maxims*).

Martha represents those in the Purgative level. Mary is entering into the Illuminative level. In this state, words and reasoning give way to intuition and the direct transmission of Jesus' divine presence. Mary can hear at this level because of the increase of her faith. Her love moves her faith to a deeper level of listening and to its fruit, interior freedom.

Lazarus: The Night of Spirit

Where is Lazarus? Did Martha in her anxiety send him out to a store for some supplies? Was he upstairs sleeping? There is not a word about him in this incident, though he was part of the household. Sometimes what the Scriptures do not say is more revealing than what they do say. Lazarus' place in the family emerges as a kind of mystery. Jesus had a word of wisdom for Martha to help her in her difficulties. He also had a word of wisdom for Mary to help her to advance. When Jesus said, "Mary has chosen the *better* part," was he not inviting her to pursue the *best* part? Thus, he was encouraging her to still greater self-surrender and trust. But there is no word of wisdom for Lazarus.

Lazarus represents not only silence but disappearance. In the Gospel of John we find out that Lazarus was suffering from a serious illness. When he becomes deathly ill, the sisters send a message to Jesus saying, "Master, the one whom you love is sick" (John 11:3). Notice the delicacy of concern that this letter communicates. It was just a statement of fact. It was not a request for a cure. It was as if they had written, "Dear Lord, here is the problem. Do what you think best." Of course, they ardently hoped that Jesus would come and cure their brother. But Jesus does not come. He deliberately waits four days. Finally he acknowledged to the disciples, "Lazarus is dead.... Now let us go to him!" Thus, he who cured thousands of others declined to make any effort to save the life of his special friend!

How are we to understand Jesus' apparent indifference? What grief and despair did Lazarus feel in his last hours, knowing that Jesus could have come and did not come? This divine action challenges our *idea* of God, our *idea* of Jesus Christ, our *idea* of the spiritual life. Surrender to the unknown marks the great transitions of the spiritual journey. On the brink of each new breakthrough there is a crisis of trust and of love.

When Jesus finally arrived at Bethany, Martha typically hurried out to meet him. Mary stayed in the house. Notice this further delicacy of love. Mary waited until she was called. Martha's prayer for Lazarus accomplished nothing. She returns to the house

21

and whispers to Mary, "The Master is here and is calling for you." Immediately Mary rises and goes to meet him.

When Mary reaches the outskirts of town where Jesus has paused, she offers exactly the same prayer that Martha made: "Lord if you had been here, my brother would not have died." Again, this is not so much a request as a statement of fact. Then Mary weeps. Jesus, seeing her tears, breaks down and bursts into tears. Tears are a most effective form of petitionary prayer. Jesus immediately enters the town and walks straight to the tomb of Lazarus. After praying to the Father, he calls out in a loud voice, "Lazarus, come forth!" That was the word of wisdom that Jesus had reserved for this supreme moment. The text reads, "And Lazarus came forth, his hands and feet bound in strips of burial cloth, and his face covered by a cloth. Jesus says to them, 'Free him and let him go.'"

What was the mysterious illness from which Lazarus suffered and died? It was the death of his false self. Death is the only cure for the false self. That is why Jesus did not come. Only the death of the false self brings liberation from the drives for survival and security, affection and esteem, and power and control, and from overidentification with a particular group or role. By overidentification with a particular group, I refer to the fact that from the

ages of four to eight we tend to interiorize unques-
tioningly the values of our parents, ethnic group,
nation, religion, peer group, television, and the Inter-
net. We may never come to reevaluate them unless
we are challenged by tragedy, illness, or some earth-
shaking event.

Jesus, through the inspirations of the Holy Spirit
and the events of daily life, speaks to us everyday,
asking us the same questions that he addressed to his
disciples in the Gospels: "What is your motive? Why
are you anxious? Why are you fearful?" We gradually learn to recognize influences that come from
our emotional programs for happiness, our temper-
amental biases, cultural prejudices, genetic make-up,
and all that opposes our embracing the full scope of
Gospel values.

Lazarus, then, is a paradigm of Christian transformation. The spiritual meaning of Lazarus for
us is that we cannot enter into the transforming
union (or heaven) with our false selves. Lazarus in
the tomb represents someone in the Night of Spirit
who feels imprisoned, forgotten by God, and abandoned by loved ones. Lazarus shows us that the
Christian journey is not a magic carpet to bliss, a
career, or a success story. It is a series of humili-
ations of the false self. Divine wisdom works both
in prayer and action to free us from the undigested
emotional junk of a lifetime that is warehoused in

the body. I have called this process of healing the "divine therapy." To make use of this term, I do not intend to bypass the traditional paradigm of friendship with Christ. The term simply adds a note that might be useful in contemporary society, especially in the West where psychological language has become almost the same as street language. The term "divine therapy" includes the great discovery by Freud about a hundred years ago of the unconscious dimension of the human psyche. Although the unconscious was intuited in times past by a number of great mystics, especially by St. John of the Cross, it was never clearly articulated or understood. Its significance for the spiritual journey is immense and crucial.

If we read John of the Cross's *Dark Night of the Soul* from the perspective of the unconscious, a remarkable light is shed on his extraordinary teaching. The Night of Spirit feels like dying. But it isn't death. It is liberation from the tyranny of the false self. It is the necessary preparation for the full transmission of divine light, life, and love. Lazarus as a symbol of Christian transformation is very close to us, and indeed is us in moments of deep purification, especially when that experience is prolonged and we feel as though there is no hope that the night will ever end. The Night of Spirit in particular is extremely searching. The Divine Therapist lovingly moderates the intensity of self-knowledge according to our state of life and capacity. Mary sitting at the feet of Jesus is only beginning the contemplative journey. Contemplation is not the reward of virtue. It is a necessity for virtue. It leads to the experience of the presence of God in pure faith. God then withdraws the divine presence, seeming to abandon us in the tomb, as it were. God returns at the appropriate time to call us forth from our darkness, confinement, loneliness, dereliction, and grief.

Jesus' loud cry ordering Lazarus to come forth from the tomb was the word of wisdom Jesus saved for him. Notice the progression that takes place as Lazarus comes forth from his entombment. He staggers to the door wrapped in burial cloths. Jesus orders, "Untie him and let him go." These words signal another stage of spiritual development. When one has emerged from the Night of Spirit, one has still to allow the Holy Spirit to work its fruits into all of one's faculties and relationships.

Every time there is significant growth in our spiritual development all our relationships change — to God, to ourselves, to other people, and to all creation. We become a new person, as did Mary of Bethany at the feet of Jesus. From this arises a new kind of activity which might be called "contemplative service." Contemplative service is service that comes from the experience of the divine indwelling —

from the Spirit living and at work within us. It is God in us serving God in others.

The divine indwelling is the doctrine that God dwells within us; hence, there is no place to go to find God. We just have to stop running away. Mary was not only assimilating God's words, she was becoming the Word of God. Each of us as a Christian is another "word-made-flesh," called to manifest Jesus Christ in our time, to our friends, family, and the people with whom we work. That is what brings the Gospel to life and builds the Christian community. The Christian community is where Jesus is experienced as a living reality. It is where people are struggling to move through the traditional stages of the spiritual journey and are supported by the presence, example, and wisdom of like-minded companions or soul-friends.

The Banquet at Bethany:
The Outpouring of Love

After the spiritual awakening of Lazarus symbolized by his resurrection from the tomb, he appears at a banquet in Simon the Leper's house (John 12:1–8). The banquet is a symbol of the celebration of the divine nuptials in someone who has moved through the trials of the Night of Spirit to the spiritual marriage, from self-centeredness to Christ-centeredness.

The account of this event manifests the deep penetration of the mystery of Christ by the author of John's Gospel. The dinner included Mary the contemplative, Martha the activist, Matthew the tax collector, Judas the thief, Simon the Leper, and Lazarus the ex-corpse. A typical Sunday congregation!

The banquet took place six days before the Passover. "Jesus was in the home of Simon the leper at Bethany. While he reclined at table a woman with an alabaster flask of pure and very costly nard perfume entered the room" (Mark 14:3–9). All eyes were fixed on her. The "very costly perfume" was the equivalent of a working man's pay for a whole year. Mary stands next to Jesus and empties the entire contents of the alabaster jar over his head! Jesus is saturated with the delicious odor as it "billowed throughout the house."

Mary's extraordinary action brought the dinner to a screeching halt. It ended all conversation. The guests could scarcely breathe, let alone eat. Everywhere was the smell of this exotic perfume. The apostles did not know what to do or say. When they finally began to get their wits together, they grumbled, "Why wasn't this perfume sold and the money given to the poor?" We are told that Judas was the spearhead of this criticism. Notice there is no comment from Lazarus. He is just present, watching all that is going on. Jesus then defends Mary:

"Let her alone. She has done this in anticipation of my burial."

Let us try to grasp the significance of Mary's gesture. For her, Jesus' body was the alabaster jar filled with the priceless perfume of the Holy Spirit. His body was to be broken so that the fullness of the Holy Spirit dwelling in him might be poured out over humanity. Just as Mary's perfume filled the whole house, the unction of the Holy Spirit, present in the precious blood of Jesus, was about to be poured out for the salvation of the world.

Mary seems to have anticipated the immense tragedy that was about to happen to Jesus in Jerusalem. For one thing she wanted to do something to show that Jesus was no ordinary guest. In the Palestinian culture, ordinary guests were anointed with oil, their feet were washed, and they were given a kiss. Such were the normal courtesies. By her act, she was affirming, "This is no ordinary guest! This is the one in whom the fullness of the Spirit of God dwells." The only way the Spirit could be fully communicated was to destroy the container. Hence, in the fervor of her grace, "she broke it," according to the text. The gesture of anointing someone was a sign of love. There was no doubt that Mary loved Jesus and that the perfume signified the gift of herself. What touched Jesus was the *totality* of her gift. Mary had reached the point where she could surrender herself to Jesus just as she was and all that she was.

Here we are at the heart of the mystery of Christianity. This is why Jesus said, "What this woman has done must be preached everywhere in the world wherever the Gospel is preached." Jesus is about to do on the cross what God the Father does for all eternity. The Father totally gives himself to his Son, transferring to him the entire riches of the godhead. What Jesus Christ did in his sacrifice on the cross was to manifest the total self-emptying of the Father, revealing in this way the inner nature of the Trinity. As the Father pours himself totally into the Son, so the Son returns all he has received to the Father. At the same time he empties himself of his divine prerogatives to become a member of the human family, even to dying on the cross.

Mary of Bethany was inspired by the Holy Spirit to express her boundless love in this dramatic and total way. In doing so, she anticipated in her own person the passion, death, and resurrection of Jesus. At the same time she manifested the unfolding of the contemplative path in all its fullness. Contemplation is not only prayer but action as well. And not only prayer and action, but the gift of one's inmost being and all that one is. We are to allow God to be God in us. Each of us is inherently capable of giving God that glory. Hence, the incredible dignity of a human person.

Lazarus is not quoted during this event. Did he recognize from his own experience that Mary had also received the transmission of unconditional love? That is who God is, and that is who we are to become.

TWO

LECTIO DIVINA

WHAT MARY OF BETHANY seems to be doing at the feet of Jesus is practicing what came to be called Lectio Divina. This Latin phrase means "reading," or more exactly "listening," to the book we believe to be divinely inspired. She is listening to Jesus' teaching. She is getting acquainted, finding out what he thinks, what he likes and does not like. We too can read Scripture to find out who Jesus is, what he likes and what he does not like. To get acquainted is to develop a personal relationship with someone towards whom we feel an attraction.

The reading of Scripture is the basis and support for all our ways of relating with God. However developed our contemplative or meditative practices may become, they still need to be nourished by Scripture. The practice of Lectio Divina is a method developed very early in Christian times. You find it in the desert fathers and mothers of the fourth century. You find it in the homilies of the fathers of the church who absorbed the teaching of Jesus and interpreted it in the light of their personal experience of relating to Jesus.

Lectio Divina is a distinct method from other contemplative practices. It is not the same as Centering Prayer or the practice of meditation taught by Dom John Main. The method of Lectio Divina has been described as methodless. A relationship with God cannot be structured or controlled. It is spontaneous. It follows the same pattern we use in getting acquainted with another human being. We have to hang out together. At first our exchanges are awkward. We make sure that our hair is parted right and our tie is on straight. We walk on eggshells lest we behave improperly or say the wrong thing.

Taking Mary of Bethany as our model we might again ask the question, "What was she doing at the feet of Jesus?" The question suggests an important principle: all prayer is related to the revelation of God in Jesus Christ. Prayer is primarily relationship. Its growth reflects the way we make friends with any person. Getting acquainted is a little awkward in the beginning. Acquaintanceship gradually moves into friendliness and familiarity. Friendliness evolves into friendship. The latter always involves a mutual commitment. Commitment may unfold into various degrees of union, like spiritual friendship or marriage.

In human relationships we feel each other out to see if going steady is a good idea. If we miss our appointments, there are consequences. But little by little we begin to feel at ease with this person. It is important to know that the other person likes us.

Gradually this evolves into the being-at-our-ease of friendliness. People at this stage begin to share their feelings with each other. They call each other up when they are upset or if they are going somewhere. They send post cards when they are traveling. As the relationship draws closer, one may even call the other person at work to say "It's just me. I wanted you to know that I am thinking of you."

Both Martha and Mary had passed through these initial levels of relationship with Jesus. Remember this was the house where he often stopped on his journeys to Jerusalem. All the members of the household had developed an ease in conversation. This happens to us when we speak to God in our own words. The more honestly we share our feelings with God, the more our relationship is likely to grow in intimacy.

True friendship is characterized by commitment. We can walk away from an acquaintance, but we cannot walk away from a friend without breaking someone's heart. As we move towards a commitment with a particular person, there is usually a crisis. We ask ourselves, "Can I share my problems and difficulties with this person? Will he keep my secrets? Will she still love me if she knows all about me?" These are important questions. One would be wise to resolve them before making a permanent commitment.

Friendship with God

Something similar happens in our relationship with God. In the beginning we say prayers that someone else has composed. Later we feel at ease in spontaneous prayer. At a certain point God invites us into a deeper commitment: to let go of the false self, to accept him as our Divine Therapist, and to show up for our daily interviews. If you don't show up regularly, a busy therapist might say, "There are plenty of other people who want my services. Please find somebody else."

Fortunately for us, God is not like this. If you miss your interviews, God says, "It's up to you. If you want to get well, come for treatment. If you're not yet ready, I'll wait for you. Come back in ten years." Meanwhile we have lost the opportunity to develop right now the special graces of the invitation.

Mary sat at the feet of Jesus listening to his words. At some point she was not listening to what he was saying. She was penetrating beyond his human characteristics and identifying with the divine Person whom her faith was intuiting and who was filling her with delight.

In the beginnings of contemplation, we are absorbed in this initial stage of meeting God at the spiritual level of our being. We feel the Spirit wants us to emphasize periods of solitude and silence when God can become present to all our faculties; not just the superficial faculties of thinking, imagination, and memory, but the spiritual faculties of intuition and will. It is a process of centering. I am not speaking of Centering Prayer as such, but the process that John of the Cross writes about in *The Living Flame of Love*. It is moving from one inner center to a deeper one, from our ordinary psychological awareness to the level of our spiritual faculties, and from the level of our spiritual faculties to our inmost being or true self. Finally, there is the moving through our inmost being into the divine presence itself which is the source out of which we emerge at every microcosmic moment of time.

Certain Buddhists have an intriguing teaching that is very friendly to the Christian idea of creation. We are coming into being, going out of it and coming back again at every split second of time. From the Judeo-Christian perspective, we are in the palm of God's hand, totally dependant on God and sustained by God's creative love at every moment. At the same time we are unique in the gifts that God has given to each of us. The practice of Lectio Divina and other practices leading to contemplation are all related to the doctrine of the divine indwelling. Moreover, it is a question not just of presence, but of action. Our relationship with God can become more and more intimate. It moves beyond friendship into various levels of union. Union can go on unfolding both in this life and for all eternity. According to St. Gregory of Nyssa, we will continue to grow in the knowledge and love of God forever. There is no completion to the human experiment. It is open-ended. There is a limit to what we can do in this body, but there may be no limit in the next life.

If we believe and hope that we are going to be living with God forever, why not get acquainted with this extraordinary presence now? In this perspective, what other things are as important as this? God's will for us is to manifest God's goodness and infinite tenderness in our lives right now. Christian tradition is not merely a handing on of various doctrines and rituals. It is the handing on of *the experience of the living Christ,* revealed in Scripture, preserved in the sacraments, renewed in every act of prayer, and present in a special way in the major events of our lives. If we are open and available to this presence, our lives will be transformed. The spiritual journey is a struggle to be ever more available to God and to let go of the obstacles to that transforming process. The Gospel is not merely an invitation to be a better person. It is an invitation to become divine. It invites us to share the interior life of the Trinity.

The Trinity, of course, is not just present in our inmost being but throughout all creation. St. Thomas Aquinas wrote, "God is existence. Hence God is present in everything that exists." The question is, What kind of presence are we dealing with? God is present to us at every level of our being. Here it is worth remembering that classical incident in chapter 12 of the Book of Numbers when Moses, the leader of the Israelites, was having administrative difficulties with Miriam and Aaron who were criticizing him. God told Moses to bring them to the Tent of Meeting. That was Moses' hangout when he was in trouble.

God said to them, "There may be among your race prophets. To one I appear in a vision. To another I reveal my thoughts in a dream. But with my servant Moses I speak mouth to mouth" — that is, being to being, without intermediary. This is the ultimate relationship with the divine.

Lectio Divina, as we saw, is a methodless method of prayer, the dynamics of which are similar to the growth of a personal relationship with anyone. Hence, we have to give time and put energy into it.

After we have investigated the other person's qualities, likes, and capacities, we have to be willing to take the plunge of trust. In the case of our relationship with Christ, we are faced with the call to discipleship and we experience a crisis of faith. We ask ourselves, "Can I really trust this God whom I have come to know so intimately? Given my circumstances, do I really want to commit myself to a life of prayer?"

The Night of Sense

The stages of acquaintanceship and friendliness normally bring us to this crisis of faith. John of the Cross calls it the Night of Sense and teaches that it happens to almost everyone who seriously undertakes the spiritual journey. God removes the sensible consolations and devotional practices that we enjoyed in the first few years. Now the liturgy is boring and uninspiring. Scripture is like reading the telephone book, ministry is a disaster, family life is full of all kinds of woes. We may suffer lawsuits, divorce, tragedy. We may have huge financial worries. Not infrequently we may ask ourselves, "Is there not a better way of getting to heaven?"

The basic issue is, "Can I trust this God enough to commit myself to a life of prayer and service?" Union with God does not normally interfere with other relationships. It simply changes our attitude towards them so that we can persevere in them, not for the sake of what we get out of them, but from a motive of unselfish love.

Contemplative prayer, which tends to stabilize in the Night of Sense, does not put other forms of prayer out of business. It simply reveals to us where they all are directed so that they actually become more meaningful. This enables us to let go of practices that were helpful in the beginning, but are no longer appropriate in the new relationship that we are developing with God.

Contemplative prayer relativizes our dependence on external practices in order to go to God. We no longer do them to placate God. Placating is a primitive kind of religious response based on an unhealthy attitude towards God. Unfortunately, God is often introduced to a child in an improper way. The fear of God is sometimes used by parents or teachers as a club in order to get children to behave. This is not good religious instruction. The best parenting is done by parents who really love each other. No education can supply that example of mutual devotion. If it is there, the seeds of a deep religious understanding are sown in children and their personal relationship to God takes on the tone that they have observed in the relationship between their mother and father. Parenting is the greatest vocation there is. Most of us are still recovering from childhood and the experience we had there. But our parents were also recovering from their childhood. This is one of the consequences of the Fall. We repeat the same mistakes that damaged us. Unless we undertake the spiritual journey seriously, we are likely to lay the same misguided trips on the next generation.

Lectio Divina leads to a personal relationship with God. The ancient monastic way of doing lectio does not mean reading a lot. It means reading the text until you feel the call of the Spirit either to reflect on a particular passage, sentence, or phrase, or to respond to the good things that you have read or heard. You may want to praise God, ask for something, or converse with God. Or you might feel like pouring out your heart to God. There is a movement from our concentrative practices to the receptive disposition that is essential for resting in God. The tradition has structured this process into sacred reading, reflecting (pondering), responding (that is, reacting with prayer), and resting in God. All these moments, so to speak, on the circle of relating to Christ are in the service of the final one, which is resting in God.

The full flowering of our relationship with God is somewhat like that of an elderly couple who have lived together for a long time, brought up the children, suffered together the ups and downs of daily life, and who really love each other. They don't have to talk all the time. They chat as they pour coffee in the morning, but they can also sit together and look at a sunset and just enjoy each other's company. They might hold hands or look into each other's eyes to maintain the sense of union. They have moved beyond conversation to communion.

This is a good symbol of what takes place in contemplative prayer. It is the capacity to give our recollected presence to God and to enjoy God's presence in return without saying anything or without trying to prove anything. We are just relishing the sense of communion, even if there is no special experience of consolation.

Lectio Divina develops spontaneously if we do not get stuck on one of the stages of the process like over-intellectualizing or the multiplication of aspirations. The heart of the prayer is to recognize the presence and action of God and to consent to it. We do not have to go anywhere; God is already with us. Effort refers to the future and to what we do not yet have. Consent refers to the present moment and its content. Faith tells us that we already have God — the divine indwelling. The most intimate relationship with God is to be completely present to God in whatever we are doing. In this sense, prayer is a preparation for life. What we do in silence under ideal circumstances, we begin to do in daily life, remaining in the interior freedom we experienced during contemplative prayer even in the midst of intense activity.

Contemplative prayer and the Seven Gifts of the Holy Spirit that manifest it are active both in prayer and action. That is the experience that Lazarus symbolizes at the banquet. All he was doing was drinking his soup and enjoying the meal. He had united his capacity for prayer and action. Once the presence of God is a permanent part of daily life, there is a sense of spaciousness in the midst of all our activities. When difficulties arise because of events or other people, and our emotional reactions start to give us trouble, we can surround them with God's presence. This awareness relativizes the importance of the compulsion that we have to do something about every situation. Yes, we have to do something about certain situations, but if we do them from false self-motivation, we will not accomplish anything. When we act from the conviction of God's presence within us and with openness to the inspirations of the Holy Spirit, action becomes effective.

The spiritual journey is very hard to initiate if we have interiorized a negative or emotionally charged idea of God in early childhood such as: "God is a tyrant who demands instant obedience. An implacable judge who is always about to bring down the verdict of guilty! Or a policeman always on the watch to catch me if I do something wrong."

This is not religious education; it is a form of terrorism. It makes God into a monster. No such God exists. The notion of God that many of us received in early childhood should be put in the wastebasket. Unfortunately, because it is emotionally charged, it keeps coming back when we start thinking of God or about the things of God. The old tapes keep replaying. "Are you sure you can trust this hazardous God?" We cannot have a profound spiritual relationship with God if we are afraid of God. The "fear of God" is a technical term in Scripture that means "cultivate the right relationship with God." And the right relationship with God is trust. In the psychological climate of our culture, we normally translate "fear" as the emotion of fear, and this is not the proper meaning of the term in Scripture.

Alcoholics Anonymous is one of the most succinct and accurate expressions of Christian spirituality. It is one of God's greatest gifts to our time. It brings many of those in recovery to a contemplative practice. Candidates for the addiction of alcoholism would save themselves and their family a lot of trouble if they seriously took up a contemplative practice. The Night of Sense, which is the ripe fruit of a regular practice of relating to God, brings us face to face with the dark side of our personality. We begin to perceive the dynamics of our unconscious, and to recognize the damage that has been done to us in early childhood. The damage may not have been deliberate, but we develop a homemade (false) self to compensate for the pain of our unfulfilled instinctual needs for security and survival, affection and esteem, and power and control. We can suppress them into the unconscious but the energy itself remains in our bodies. Then all through our lives, unless we undertake the spiritual journey or undergo deep psychotherapy, we remain unaware of the intense power that that energy continues to exert over our actions and in our decision-making processes.

For example, some people marry because they want to have the mother who loved them in childhood. They are looking for somebody to do their laundry and a shoulder to cry on like mama used to provide. Or they are looking for the father they never had. They may marry a person whom they think they love, but secretly they are looking for the healing of a wound that was never acknowledged. This marriage is in trouble from the beginning because when your spouse finds that you married her or him because he or she was a father or mother figure, he or she is going to say, "I didn't marry you for that." People can also enter religious life because they never had a family, and a religious community may look like it would provide one. It is a family in the broad sense, but not the one they are expecting. No one is going to sit you on his or her lap and sing lullabies to put you to sleep.

Traditional practices and devotions are not always *the* tradition. They may be just something people have done for centuries and may never have thought of changing. In recent centuries, mental prayer has been presented as stages or states each of which takes a long time to negotiate. First there was discursive meditation, usually reflection on some text of Scripture or from a spiritual book. That was followed by a long period in which affective prayer predominated: the multiplication of explicit acts of the will in the form of aspirations. If you lived long enough, you might have a few moments of contemplative prayer or resting in God. This was a "false tradition." It became so formalized that if anybody regularly said grace at meals or night prayers, or went to Mass a couple of times a week, they were encouraged to enter a cloister.

Christian contemplation unfolds from the seeds of the graces planted at baptism. Among these are the Seven Gifts of the Spirit, all of which are oriented towards contemplative prayer and its development. Ordinarily, the Fruits of the Spirit appear first: charity, joy, peace, meekness, gentleness, long-suffering, goodness, patience, self-control (Gal. 5:23). If we are developing our friendship with Christ, these fruits are bound to appear. If they do not, we can question the seriousness or the depth of the relationship that we are having with Christ.

But Lectio Divina is not a series of steps or stages as has been presented in recent centuries: reading, reflecting, responding, and resting. It doesn't work that way, although it could be a good way to learn it. Lectio is a dynamic relationship with God in which you may read, reflect, respond, or rest, all in the same period of prayer. Those four moments are like moments on a circle, not rungs on a ladder. By beginning at any moment on that circle, we are in relationship with all the other moments. The nature of lectio is to soften up and train all our faculties, so that each in its own way can enter fully into the spiritual movement towards divine union. Resting in God is not some abstract state but rather the full flowering of the potential of all our faculties to relate to Christ in their own way.

We can start people at any one of those four moments. If they have not had the experience of discursive meditation, the Spirit will see what is missing in their journey and simply lead them to it during the time of lectio. This is what happened in the Centering Prayer movement. At the time it began, I was concerned about offering in the marketplace a Christian method that would be comparable to the methods of our Hindu, Buddhist, and Islamic brothers and sisters. In the 1970s very few were coming to Christian monasteries while many — 10,000 every summer according to some estimates — were going to India in search of a guru. They did not find comparable spirituality in the Christian tradition either in catechism classes, high school, college, the local parish, or even in religious life. This seemed to me to be tragic because through my studies and experience in the monastery, I realized the rich treasures that the Christian contemplative heritage possessed. I knew it was also a necessary base for interreligious dialogue and a source of unity among Christian denominations. Contemplative prayer crosses over doctrinal differences and emphasizes the essentials of the Christian religion, which is the lived experience of Christ and the love for others that flows from that experience.

After a few years a number of people practicing Centering Prayer spontaneously became interested in Lectio Divina. They asked what it was and wanted to know how to do it. In many groups, there is a period of lectio during the weekly meeting after the group has practiced Centering Prayer. Scripture supports contemplative prayer through the discipline of lectio. Without some such support, our prayer can get dried out and stagnate.

Our personal experience of prayer also finds apt expression in the symbols of Scripture. If we speak from the experience of resting in God, the gift of wisdom enables us to choose examples and symbols from Scripture that help to explain our experience to ourselves and to other people. Resting in God makes all the difference between preaching that comes out of love and preaching as an academic exposition of truths, however useful, which only engages the mind but does not touch hearts. Lectio Divina and contemplative prayer lead to a transmission of the living Christ beyond words and concepts. As John of the Cross writes, "The dogmas of the faith are like the shining surfaces of the ocean. They point to the mystery that lies beneath but they cannot provide the experience of that mystery." Like Peter, we have to launch out into the deep and let down our nets for a catch.

THREE

THE EUCHARIST

L ET'S RETURN TO MARY OF BETHANY. She was listening to the teaching of Jesus. She had reflected
on it and responded to it, and now she was communing with it and resting in it. The four moments
of relating to Christ through the external word of
God are all designed to awaken us to the interior
word of God, the divine presence that has always
been there. It is waiting for us. We can be awakened
to it by listening at ever-deepening levels to the word
of God.

As a result of listening to the Person of the Word
beyond the visible presence of Jesus and his speech,
she was "being assimilated" to God. In other words,
she was becoming the word of God. This is the dynamic process of lectio: it changes us into the word
of God so that we become a kind of fifth gospel by
manifesting in our time and place the values of the

Gospel to the people we know and love. Above all, we make tangible the presence of Jesus living in us in his glorified body and through the Holy Spirit. Our minds and hearts and all our other faculties have been refined over time by the process of lectio so that they are now habitually docile to the movements of the Spirit.

There is another aspect to *becoming* the word of God that is important. It joins together contemplative prayer and contemplative service so that one is resting even in the midst of activity. This is to do what God does. God is always at rest and always creating at the same time, and yet beyond both.

Contemplative prayer, however profound, is not the perfect reflection or full manifestation of God. Nor does action, however effective from a human point of view, manifest God. It is only when the two are habitually working together that we have made significant progress. At that point we become an apostle in our very being, not only in what we say or do. We are apostles in the sense of being immersed in the infusion of divine love that the apostles received at Pentecost, which is the way the early fathers of the church understood it. We transmit the Gospel more by who we are and how we love than by any other means. All rituals, prayers, and sacraments further this transforming movement so that we can be Christ in every moment. Then we manifest the infinite tenderness of God whether we are sleeping or awake, eating or walking down the street, doing household chores or counseling. Such persons pour into all their relationships and even into the atmosphere the energy of divine love and compassion.

With regard to the dynamic process of Lectio Divina, the four moments of relating to Christ at the center of the circle are the focus of each period of lectio. When we take up the Scriptures and begin to read, we may stop after the first line or even after the first word. Normally, however, we read a passage and pause when we feel an attraction to a particular sentence or phrase. It is not a question of thinking *about* the text, but of simply *thinking the text*. This gives the Holy Spirit the chance to teach us how to listen to the particular text at ever deeper levels as well as to move with great ease and freedom to other moments on the circle of Lectio Divina to which the Spirit may attract us.

That is why to do lectio in common is not the traditional way of doing Lectio Divina. The very nature of Lectio Divina is its spontaneity or unstructured character. Whenever we partake of any kind of prayer in common, there has to be some structure. Lectio in common is a way of sharing the word of God. It can be extremely supportive and inspiring, but Lectio Divina is primarily designed for private consumption. The Spirit then deals with each of us where we are in our life of prayer right now. This is not possible when we are reflecting on the text, responding to it in prayer, or resting with it in silence for a specific period of time, normally for a couple of minutes. This is a good practice for getting acquainted with Scripture for those who have little knowledge of it, and with the members of the prayer group. It is also a good way to prepare for the Sunday liturgy.

Now let us look at one other great practice that brings us into the presence of God. In the Second Vatican Council's *Constitution on the Sacred Liturgy* we hear about four presences of Christ in the Eucharist.

The first presence of Christ in the Eucharistic Liturgy is the gathering of the assembly. "Wherever two or three people are gathered together," Jesus promised, "there am I in the midst of you." So before the priest makes any gesture or even greets the community, Christ is present. This first presence has significant implications for ecumenical gatherings. It means that at least at that point everyone is united in Christ. Where did he come from? Where did he come from when he visited the apostles on the night of his resurrection and appeared suddenly in their midst, despite locked doors. Perhaps he came out of their hearts where he was living already! In any case, when as a community we come to a eucharistic celebration, we are united in Christ. The mysterious but real presence of Christ in his glorified body emerges from the community as it gathers for prayer before the participants have said a word.

The second presence identified by the council fathers is the formal proclamation of the Gospel. Perhaps you have seen processions to the lectern in which the Gospel book is held over the head of the deacon and there are incense, bows, and other rituals. According to the document of the council, Christ is present in a special way when the Gospel is proclaimed in the worshiping assembly. In view of this, the Gospel should not be proclaimed by anybody who happens to pick up the book. Liturgical readers are encouraged to prepare the text and read it in such a way that the presence of Christ is transmitted through their voice, demeanor, and understanding of the text.

It was through this presence that St. Anthony of Egypt received his monastic vocation. He went into a local parish church one day and heard the Gospel text, "If you want to be my disciple, go and sell all you have, give it to the poor, and come follow me." He understood these words to be addressed directly to him. The Gospel, when it is proclaimed, addresses the heart of each individual person in the assembly. There is a message for us each time it is read.

The Gospel when it is proclaimed has the characteristic that the apostle Paul called a word of wisdom. A word of wisdom is not just a wise saying. It can be a casual remark or even a joke, but it resonates in one's heart, and one knows intuitively that God has spoken. It may suggest that it is time to change something in one's life. Maybe there is some reconciliation that needs to be attempted.

A thousand years after Anthony, St. Francis of Assisi heard the same text. He too went out and sold everything he had. If the message goes to your heart, you can be sure you can do what it says. That is the specific difference between an exhortation and a word of wisdom. We have a lot of good ideas that we would like to carry out. There are lots of self-help programs that might help us. But a word of wisdom *is* empowering and according to this text of the council, is available whenever the Gospel is proclaimed. The reception of the divine message normally depends on the minister to communicate the power that is there. That is part of the mystery of redemption. We are invited to share in the mystery of Christ's redeeming passion, death, and resurrection.

The third presence noted by the fathers of the council is the eucharistic prayer in which the glorified body of Christ becomes present on the altar. Christ who is present in the community and in the proclamation of the Gospel becomes bodily present in the Eucharist and gives himself to the community as a whole.

The fourth presence takes place when the presence of Christ on the altar is communicated to the community one by one. This is the way that personal redemption takes place. Redemption is not mass produced; it happens one person at a time. As each member of the congregation receives Communion, the glorified body of Christ enters into his or her inmost being. The species of bread and wine that are brought forward at the Offertory represent ourselves, indeed the total gift of ourselves like Mary of Bethany's total gift of herself. God wants *us,* not so much what we can do or what we can say. During the time that the sacred species of bread and wine are subject to the digestive process we are physically the temples of the glorified Christ. Notice the ascending levels of presence, the movement from what is external and general to what is most intimate and particular.

Unfortunately, the council fathers did not go on to the fifth presence. Although it is implied in the document, it is not explicit.

What is the fifth presence of Christ in the Eucharist? It is the presence that Mary of Bethany attained through the dynamic process of listening in Lectio Divina and of assimilating and being assimilated by the Word of God. The Eucharist received in Holy Communion awakens us to the permanent presence of Christ within us at the deepest level. The

Eucharist, like the Word of God in Scripture, has as its primary purpose to bring us to the awareness of God's abiding presence within us. In these five presences of Christ we find the same movement towards union with God that we noticed in Lectio Divina.

Contemplative prayer, of course, has the same movement. It reduces the obstacles to the transforming energy of the Eucharist so that we can manifest in our attitudes and behavior the living Christ within us. As Jesus said, "He that loves me will in turn be loved by my Father; and I will love him and will manifest myself to him" (John 14:21). This text refers to this fifth level of presence. A contemplative practice is not dissociated or separate from the dynamic movement of lectio and the sacraments. If we do not have a discipline to reduce the obstacles in us to experiencing the presence of God, the full power of the sacraments are diluted and do not achieve their full potential to transform us. That is why some people can receive Communion every day for years and remain unchanged. They do not make a serious effort to face the obstacles in themselves. They crave security and power, affection and esteem, and unstinting approval. If one person dislikes them, they may have to go to a rehab center for a month to recover. They demand to have control over everything and everybody in their lives. They are upset if somebody opposes them even in trivial details. Perhaps you know somebody like this. There is usually one in every family or workplace. Maybe you are one of them! But even if we are not a classical example of these childish drives, we all bring with us something of the frustrations of early childhood. Our ways of dealing with them are rooted in us by our endless efforts to find happiness as we grow up without the experience of God's presence.

The fact is, we are all in desperate need of happiness and don't know where it can be found. This teaching is classical in the Christian tradition and is described in theology as the consequences of original sin. Contemporary psychology has given us a detailed diagnosis of what this means.

The first consequence of original sin, according to traditional theology, is illusion. We don't know what true happiness is or where it is to be found. The second is concupiscence. Since we are made for boundless happiness, we have to find it somewhere and not knowing where to find it, we look for it in the wrong places. And third, we suffer from weakness of will, which means that even if someday we discover where true happiness is to be found, our will is too weak to do anything about it. This is why we need to be redeemed. It is not going to happen through our own efforts. What we can do is to recognize our dilemma. This is the great truth that those in Alcoholics Anonymous and its associated programs know. Contemplative prayer brings us to the same realization through the ongoing experience of self-knowledge.

The first step of AA is to acknowledge that our lives have become "unmanageable." That is the conviction that comes through understanding the consequences of original sin from bitter experience. Our will is too weak to recover from the deep-seated drives of our emotional programs for happiness that become centers of gravity around which everything in our lives revolves. Our emotional reactions to events and persons circulate around these energy centers like planets around the sun. Anything entering into our private universe is judged on the basis of this question: "Is this good for *my* programs for happiness or not?"

The presences of Christ in the Eucharist are incredibly powerful, but thwarted unless we are also working at the spiritual journey through the process of dismantling our emotional programs for happiness and our overidentification with the beliefs of our group. Where is the violence in the world today coming from? It is coming from the frustrated emotional programs of innumerable people who are pouring negative energy into their communities and into the global atmosphere. The peace that Jesus promised through the power of his resurrection is unknown to them.

Contemplative prayer is life under the influence of the Seven Gifts of the Spirit. There are three contemplative gifts: wisdom, understanding, and knowledge. There are four gifts for the active life: reverence, counsel, fortitude, and piety. Normally, it is in prayer and silence that we encounter the space to perceive the damage done to us in early childhood or that we have done to ourselves.

According to recent authors on the subject of co-dependency, ninety-eight percent of the population, at least in the West, is co-dependent or comes from a dysfunctional family. That statistic is approaching the universal character of the consequences of original sin: we have only two more percentage points to go. In effect, just about everybody in the human family suffers from the consequences of original sin and does not know what to do about it. Meanwhile, we carry out in daily life the habitual patterns, necessary in early childhood to survive, but totally inappropriate for adults.

If control is our principal idea of what happiness is, we think, "Oh, how happy I would be if I could only control this situation ... if I could only control my daughter's marriage ... if I could only be sure that my son gets into his father's profession ... if I could only get out of this relationship." The history of the world provides many examples of persons who could never have enough power. The unlimited character of the emotional programs for happiness comes from the fact that they emerged at a time when there was no reason in our infant psyches to moderate them. Feelings and instincts are not wrong, but in early childhood reason is not present to moderate them. Hence they grow in wild exaggeration.

In the deep rest of contemplative prayer the human body receives permission, so to speak, to evacuate the emotional junk of a lifetime. In other words, we have a psychological tummy filled with emotional traumas. We are like persons sitting for ten, twenty, thirty, or forty years, on a meal that we never digested. The best remedy is not an antacid, but a good vomit! What we need to do to heal our psychological indigestion is a thorough evacuation of the emotional trauma itself. That requires a willingness to feel the primitive emotions of grief, fear, panic, despair, or whatever emotions accompanied the traumatic events or situations of early life. In the purification of the unconscious this healing takes place through the process of contemplative prayer. Contemplative prayer gradually brings about the liberation of whatever prevents the presence of God from becoming a part of our constant awareness. Through the Seven Gifts of the Spirit, especially the gift of knowledge, the emotional programs that we counted on to bring us happiness are relativized. We are beginning to taste what true happiness really is. It is the experience of God loving us into existence.

If the Lamb of God has taken away all our sins, as is proclaimed at every Mass, where are they? They exist only in our memory. As soon as we are sorry for our sins, they are gone. Guilt feelings are harmful. There is true guilt when we do something wrong, but if it lasts more than fifteen or twenty seconds, it is probably neurotic. It reflects our disappointment at not showing up as holy or as nice as we had imagined ourselves to be.

Three basic theological principles underlie every Christian contemplative practice. We will look at the first two in this chapter. The first is the firm conviction of faith in the divine indwelling. In the practice of Centering Prayer we put ourselves in the presence of God and consent to God's presence and action within us. We consent to the fact that from the instant of our creation, the divine Trinity, Father, Son, and the Holy Spirit, have been dwelling in us as the source of our being at every level. The three Persons of the Trinity relate to us twenty-four hours a day. Thus, contemplative prayer is Trinitarian in its source.

Secondly, contemplation is Christological in its focus. We commit ourselves to the process of the liberation of our conscious and unconscious motivation. We open to the contemplative gifts of the Spirit that are the source of contemplative prayer. Our suffering and our joys in this prayer are a participation in Christ's passion, death, and resurrection.

If we pray with the intention to open and surrender to God, drawing the curtains on our ordinary thinking processes for a specified time like half an hour, we are responding to Christ's call to repentance; that is, to change the direction in which we are searching for happiness. We are accepting Christ's invitation to a daily interview with him as the Divine Therapist. Through this profoundly psycho-spiritual process, the Spirit works back through our personal life history. Like an archaeological dig, beginning where we are now, the Spirit explores our personal life histories layer by layer — back through adulthood, adolescence, childhood, early childhood, and infancy. Every now and then, the Spirit gives us a breather, a plateau on which to work new insights into all our relationships. Every time we move to a new level of faith and self-knowledge, all our relationships change: to ourselves, others, nature, the cosmos, and above all to God. When that work is completed, the Spirit seems to say, "Let's move on to the next level." Thus we access each level until we come to the bottom where the real source of most of our emotional problems actually is, the fragility of early childhood.

The psychological experience of contemplative prayer often feels as if we are getting worse. Actually, we are only getting in touch with our basic problems — the primitive emotions that set off the elaborate defense apparatus that as infants and young children we devised in order to survive. When we sit in Centering Prayer, introduce our sacred symbol, and enter a certain degree of rest, our defenses go down. The growth of interior silence along with our growing trust in God, enables us to face the dark side of our personality. We know that God knows us through and through, and still loves us. In fact, God could not be more delighted to provide this information. Grace enables us to evacuate negative emotions that are stuck in our nervous system, hindering the free flow of pure love that leads to divine transformation.

In contemplative prayer we are identifying ourselves with the passion of Jesus who took upon himself all the sins of the world. As Paul writes, "God made him to be sin for our sake" (2 Cor. 5:21) — not just our personal sins, but the tendencies to sin that are called the capital sins. These flow from the habitual frustration of our emotional programs for happiness when the events of daily life contradict our demands or expectations.

In sharing Christ's passion and death in contemplative prayer, we may feel endless dryness or at times a bombardment of thoughts. We experience primitive emotions as did St. Thérèse of Lisieux who went through this profound purification even though she was so young. Thérèse wrote, "I accept the wildest thoughts that go through my imagination, for the love of God." We need to cultivate a friendly attitude towards this garbage because otherwise we might try to push these painful emotions back into the unconscious. If we let the emotional junk come to consciousness, it will pass through our awareness into the atmosphere and be gone forever. All we have to do is to wave good-bye.

Sometimes in the midst of the unloading process, something serious comes up like rejection or abuse that needs psychological help. Psychotherapists who understand the spiritual journey are a necessary support in these circumstances. There needs to be a fruitful symbiosis between spiritual direction and psychotherapy.

Dryness in prayer and the sense of abandonment by God are a participation in the passion of Christ. After each humiliation of the false self, we get closer to the sources of the problems of early life, perhaps even as far back as the womb. Every time we move down in humility, we instantly move to a new level of freedom. The spiral staircase winds up as well as down. We experience inner resurrections. The resurrection of Jesus manifests itself through the Fruits of the Holy Spirit: charity, joy, peace, and the rest. Then at a more profound level the Seven Gifts of the

Spirit manifest in acts inspired by the Beatitudes. The movement of humility and the movement of transformation proceed at the same time. Sometimes one predominates over the other. In the end they seem to come together in a disposition of utter humility.

The fruit of Mary's sitting at the feet of Jesus in contemplative prayer is the insight that she manifested when she poured the precious perfume, symbol of the Spirit, over the head of Jesus at the house of Simon the Leper. While manifesting the total gift of herself, there remains for her and for us the mysterious passage from union to unity. This passage consists of losing one's very self for the love of God. In the movement towards unity with God we have to let go of the self as a fixed point of reference. The Greek fathers called this process divinization. This does not mean that we disappear into the Absolute like a drop of water in the ocean. Rather, we become the whole universe when there is no "I" to prevent it. Although we still maintain our uniqueness as God's eternal gift, there is no possessiveness, no attachment; there is just freedom.

We might distinguish four stages of interior freedom: freedom from sin, freedom from the tendency of sin, freedom to love, and finally just freedom — freedom to be what God wants us to be in the present moment without reflection on self because there is no self to come back to.

When Mary of Bethany spread the perfume of incredible value over the head of Jesus, she anticipated his passion and death. His sacred body contained the perfume of infinite sweetness. The blood of Christ poured forth from his body broken on the cross is a vivid symbol of the total gift of the Father, of all that the Father is, which is the Son. The blood of Christ symbolizes the supreme gift of the Spirit poured out without measure over the world.

The Buddha, towards the end of his life, gathered together eighty thousand disciples, monks who had been working vigorously on the spiritual journey. When they had all settled down, the Buddha lifted up a lotus flower, the symbol in his teaching of the highest attainment of enlightenment. As all the monks gazed on the lotus flower, they were moved into a state of ecstatic absorption in which they forgot themselves completely and entered into unity with all creation. The vast mountain valley was filled with an incredible depth of silence. All of a sudden, a monk standing near the Buddha started to laugh: "Ah-ha-ha-ha-ha-ha!" His laughter echoed off the mountain peaks and left all the other monks in a state of stunned shock. How could anybody do such a thing at such a sacred time? The Buddha, undisturbed, slowly lowered the lotus flower. Immediately he turned to the monk and imparted to him the Dharma, that is, the fullness of enlightenment.

The Buddha evidently recognized that this man had attained something beyond the state of oneness that all the other monks had achieved. This monk, by his spontaneous laughter, manifested that he had transcended every means of relating to ultimate reality. He did not need any human experience, support, or ritual to sustain it. He had discovered who he was. He had become ultimate reality, not theologically, but experientially. This is the grace that Mary of Bethany manifested at the banquet at the house of Simon the Leper. In emptying the jar of perfume over the head and body of Jesus she revealed that she understood the profound significance of the passion and death of Christ. She had assimilated the mystery of redemption and was expressing her identification with it.

As we progress in the spiritual journey there are surprises. In general, we only know that they will lead where Jesus invited us to go. "Follow me," he said. Where is Jesus going? To Jerusalem, Calvary, hell, and finally into the bosom of the Father. In that place we do not need anything else. Once we have given ourselves totally to God, all that God is and has is ours. God is unconditional love and when we are unconditional love, in some way, we too are God. That is the invitation of the Gospel and the ultimate purpose of every kind of ministry, service, ritual, and sacrament. Jesus said, "Little children, here is the kingdom. It is all yours." How do we receive it? Not by striving for it, but by consenting to it. Jesus said in another place, "If you want to save your life, you will bring yourself to ruin. But if you bring yourself to nothing, you will find out who you are" (Mt. 10:39). When we are no thing, no role, no emotional program for happiness, no fixed point of reference, we too are unconditional love.

 FOUR

THE CONTEMPLATIVE DIMENSION OF THE GOSPEL

IN PREVIOUS CHAPTERS I described the practice of contemplative prayer as a participation in the Paschal Mystery — the passion, death, and resurrection of Jesus. I related this to the process of Lectio Divina, one of the oldest forms of meditative practice in the Christian religion, and then to the Eucharist. Contemplative prayer is in continuity with both the movement of Lectio Divina and the five presences of Christ in the Eucharist.

Contemplative prayer prepares us for a more profound reception of the Eucharist. It enables us to bring the fruits of prayer and the sacraments into daily life so that our entire being is more and more saturated with the divine presence and the concerns of the Gospel. Justification by faith is not just a cloak to put on. It is the deep interior transformation of everything in us into the mind and heart of Christ.

Contemplation Builds Christian Community

In the last chapter we looked at the first two theological principles on which contemplative prayer in the Christian tradition rests. A third principle is also important. Any practice moving towards contemplation is ecclesial in its effects. It bonds the people who are doing it with everybody else who is doing a similar practice, and indeed with everyone else in the human family. It creates community. As we sit in silence, we realize our oneness with others, not only with those with whom we pray, but with everyone on earth — past, present, and to come. What is deepest in them, their oneness with the divine presence, resonates with what is deepest in us. Hence, their joys, their trials, and their openness to God are part of us. In this way we share each other's burdens, as Paul says.

In contemplative practice, as we pray together identifying ourselves with the Paschal Mystery, we believe that Christ is in the center of the circle imparting to each the special graces each one needs. The participants are pooling their silence, so to speak, so that everyone gathered there can drink from this marvelous well of living water that rises up from the center of the circle. Silence in this context is liturgy of an exalted kind. We do not say or do anything, but we engage in a special kind of action that might be called alert receptivity. It is opening and consenting to God's presence and action within us.

The method of meditation as taught by John Main and the Centering Prayer method of contemplation are not so much something new in the Christian tradition as something old that is being renewed. The contemplative dimension of the Gospel has always been there but not as explicitly as it is now. Time tends to bring out the implications of the Christian message. The Spirit adjusts to people at different times and places in history. That is why the Spirit likes a little elbow room and does not like to be limited by excessive structures. When there is a reform of ecclesiastical structures, the Spirit rushes in. When the Spirit stirs up a big wind like the one occurring at Pentecost or during the Second Vatican Council, the wind in its turn may stir up a lot of dust. Things may happen concomitantly that are not always the direct intention of the Spirit. They may be overreactions to a prior sense of rigidity or overconfinement. Like anybody who has been confined, when you get out, you start to run.

The movement towards contemplative prayer responds to an enormous spiritual hunger in the human family. There is a huge vacuum in the world today because the Christian religion lost its hold on the masses after the French Revolution and throughout the Industrial Revolution of the nineteenth century. Science, or more exactly scientism, which had become a kind of replacement for Christianity, got knocked into a cocked hat by two world wars and the cold war. It is no longer a substitute for religion or a panacea for unlimited progress, as was blissfully thought to be the case fifty or a hundred years ago.

As a result of these historical developments, people today are looking not so much for doctrinal certitude as for meaning in life. This need is greatly increased by the information explosion, a horizontal expansion towards unlimited information without a corresponding vertical dimension of meaning. We need an explosion of meaning if we are to handle this explosion of information in a fully human way. It is not surprising that people, prompted by the grace of God, are thinking, "How does one live in a world where neither science nor religion are meeting the needs of people at the deepest level?"

This awareness seems to be a movement of the Holy Spirit. It needs to be given a chance to grow and to follow its own momentum. It has already initiated a growing sense of oneness beyond doctrinal differences among members of the Christian main-line churches. One of the purposes of the Centering Prayer movement as of the Christian Meditation Community is to contribute to the renewal of the Christian contemplative tradition and to make it available to the people of every Christian denomination. We all have roots in the early Christian centuries when the contemplative tradition was much more vigorous than it has been in the past few centuries.

John of the Cross is one of the major exponents of Christian mysticism. He teaches that contemplation begins in the Night of Sense, which brings to an end the springtime of the spiritual life. We experience, in some degree, the absence of God so that the practices that used to bring us satisfaction, enthusiasm, and motivation for ministry and the service of others, dry up. During this extended period of dryness, there is a disconcerting sense of going backwards in the spiritual journey. At the same time we experience a desire for solitude and a disinclination or inability to meditate discursively. We no longer can move from one concept to the next as in discursive meditation or multiply acts of the will as in affective prayer.

Lectio, as we saw, consists of four moments or ways of relating to Christ. The practice prepares our faculties to enter into deeper relationship with Christ. Our faculties become oriented towards resting in God. Rest, however, is not the end. It is rather the beginning of an even more intimate relationship with Christ in which the contemplative dimension is the source of our activity. No longer does the false self, with its dependence on our emotional programs for happiness, overidentification with our group, and cultural conditioning motivate what we do.

When we reflect in our prayer and multiply particular acts of the will, we are dominating the conversation. But if we really believe in the divine indwelling and the promptings of the Spirit, we are more apt to listen. And the more we listen, the more we realize that the inspirations of the Spirit have to be *heard*. We cease to drown them out with our brilliant flights of metaphysics, theology, devotion, or whatever we think is prayer.

John of the Cross was greatly influenced by the sixth-century Syrian monk, Pseudo Dionysius, about whom we know practically nothing. He had an enormous influence on Christian spirituality because he identified himself as a disciple of Paul. In those days plagiarism was not considered a fault. When authors wanted their material to be well circulated, they piggybacked on one of the saints or apostles. That is what Pseudo Dionysius did. His teaching is in turn reflected in *The Cloud of Unknowing*, by a fourteenth-century anonymous English mystic. *The Cloud* modifies the overintellectual tendency of Pseudo Dionysius while giving us at the same time his profound teaching.

John of the Cross used the works of Pseudo Dionysius in Spanish translation as his bedside reading.
The research of Marilyn May Mallory, a professor
in the Netherlands who did a survey on contemplative prayer about twenty-five years ago, has shown
that in one point at least there is a serious mistransla-
tion of the original text.[1] According to the translation
that John of the Cross used, the text read, "We must
be detached *from* all our desires in order to reach
divine union." To be detached from every desire is
virtually impossible in a monastery. It is absolutely
impossible for those who live in the world. But that
is not what Pseudo Dionysius actually wrote. The
correct translation is that we must be detached *in* all
our desires. This is obviously a whole other world
of meaning. But for three or four centuries gener-
ous people, pursuing the contemplative life, have
been frustrated and confused by John of the Cross's
injunction to give up every single desire. Contemplative prayer gives us the grace to be detached *in* our
desires. That means that our desires must be freed
from the motivation of the false self. Then we can
lead the spiritual life in any state of life as normal
human beings.

John of the Cross is a brilliant observer of the psy-

---

1. Marilyn May Mallory, *Christian Mysticism Transcending Techniques*
(Assen, The Netherlands: Van Gorcum).

chological experience of contemplative prayer, but he comes with some limitations. Even the saints and mystics cannot be read with absolute confidence. We have to bring a certain critical judgment to what we read. In the beginning of the spiritual journey we don't have the foundation necessary to be critical, but as time goes on we get some experience of our own. Then, if some text does not hit us quite right, we need to see if there might not be another and clearer explanation.

The following text is one of the prime sources for any practice leading to contemplative prayer: "If you wish to pray, go into your private room, shut the door and pray to your Father in secret and your Father who sees in secret will reward you" (Matthew 6:6). This is a wisdom saying of enormous importance and has consequences for those interested in contemplative prayer. It is the clarion call to listen and to be open to the divine indwelling.

Abba Isaac was interviewed by a traveler from the West named John Cassian. The latter visited the monasteries of Egypt in the fourth century and gathered wisdom sayings of the elders into a book called the *Conferences of Cassian*. He then took them back to the West and founded a Western monastery. This tradition filtered into the Rule of St. Benedict, the rule that almost all the contemplative orders of men in the West have followed to the present day.

Here is Abba Isaac's advice to Cassian[2] — little did he know that he was speaking to someone who would affect the next two thousand years of seekers. Says Abba Isaac, "We need to be especially careful to follow the Gospel precept which instructs us to go into our private room and shut the door, so that we may pray to our Father. And this is how we do it."

Here we find a method offered in the fourth century that answers an objection often raised today, that contemplative prayer cannot be achieved through a method. True, it cannot be achieved by a method alone, but neither can it be achieved without a method unless by God's special intervention. There are different methods of preparing for contemplation, but they all go back to the words of Jesus himself, at least as interpreted by someone who walked the spiritual path for many years in extreme solitude and in a community of seekers.

This is Abba Isaac's commentary. "We pray in our private room whenever we withdraw our hearts completely from the tumult and noise of our thoughts and our worries and when secretly and intimately we offer our prayers to the Lord."

Abba Isaac is obviously talking metaphorically. Few had a private room in Jesus' time. Anyone who

---

2. Conference Nine.

had a roof over his head was well-to-do. The term "private room" is a metaphor for the spiritual level of our being. This is a private place beyond the flow of our ordinary psychological awareness, with its endless stream of thoughts, commentaries, and emotional reactions to events taking place in daily life or regurgitated in our memory.

In the method proposed by Jesus, we leave outside for the time of prayer not just the environment, other people, and outside activities, but our thoughts, perceptions, worries, and plans — "the tumult and noise of our thoughts," as Abba Isaac put it. We are to cultivate interior silence and the spiritual level of our being, that is, our spiritual will to God and our passive intellect, which is able to know things by intuition. Abba Isaac continues, "We pray with the door shut when without opening our mouths and in perfect silence, we offer our petitions to the one who pays no attention to words but looks hard at our hearts."

No amount of spiritual "yakking" can take the place of the intention to be with God at the deepest level of our being. This movement into our private room, into the innermost part of our being, is a movement of opening to the divine indwelling. The divine indwelling is the fundamental principle of relating to God in the Christian life, whether we are in prayer or action.

Abba Isaac continues, "We pray in secret, when in our hearts alone and in our recollected spirits." Notice the word "recollected." This prayer is not an afternoon nap. It is not a magic carpet to bliss or a tête à tête with a warm fuzzy. This prayer is getting down to business; it is the movement of faith towards the divine indwelling. Faith is a conviction. Love is a choice, an intention, that enables us to be recollected in interior silence. It prevents the silence from becoming a mental vacuum. We do not make our minds a blank. Rather, we deliberately open ourselves to God whom we believe is present in our inmost being.

Notice that we are to pray in "our hearts alone." The heart, in the desert tradition, represents the will or our inmost being. An alert receptivity is the proper attitude. The Abba continues, "We address God and reveal our wishes only to Him and in such a way that the hostile powers themselves have no inkling of their nature."

This last statement requires a brief commentary regarding the understanding of people of this period. The fathers and mothers of the desert believed that if we are thinking during prayer, the devil can perceive what we are thinking about. In this way he can plan a strategy to suggest thoughts and temptations that will pull us out of the movement towards interior silence. He seeks to draw us out of our private room and back into the tumult and noise of our ordinary psychological awareness. Thus, when we are praying to the Father in secret, it is as if we must hide — hide from others, hide from our thoughts, and hide from ourselves.

The desert mothers and fathers identified the hostile powers as demons and the devil as their chief. They even developed nicknames for them because of their frequent interaction with them. They used to call the devil, "the old boy." In the desert tradition, when somebody gets serious about the spiritual life, the devil gets very nervous. For most of us he just rolls over and goes back to sleep. The activity of our false selves is enough to keep us preoccupied and miserable. But when people become serious about the spiritual journey, the devil is in danger of losing his power over a vast multitude of people.

We find a similar insight in Hindu and Buddhist spirituality as well. Those who are on the spiritual path are pouring positive energy into the atmosphere, which can heal people, even at a distance. Thus if one actually dismantles the false self and becomes a vessel of divine love, the devil is in tough shape. One might wrestle from him a whole neighborhood — or the whole world, for that matter — depending on how powerful one's prayer and how completely divine love takes over one's life. Anthony, having conquered the devils and having reached the transforming union, retired to an abandoned fort full of all kinds of reptiles, symbols in the popular mind of the time of the demons. The fort you might say, represented the military industrial complex of the demons. Through the power of his prayer, he returned the area to peace and opened it up to the reign of God.

John of the Cross says that the hostile powers cannot interfere when we are recollected on the spiritual level of our being. They can't figure out what we are doing.

What are we praying for in "utter silence"? If we are not supposed to open our mouths or to request anything particular by way of petition, what precisely are we doing? Here again the Gospel comes to our rescue with clear instructions. Jesus says in Matthew 7:9, "Which one of you, if your child asks you for a piece of bread, will give him or her a stone?"

In Palestine at that period bread was flat, like pita bread today, so it looked like a stone. Thus a malicious parent could say, "Here Sonny, have a nice piece of bread," and it turns out to be a rock! Or again, "What parent if a child asked for a fish, would give him or her a snake?" In the Sea of Galilee there are fish that look like snakes. A malicious parent could say, "Dear child, you want a fish? Try this poisonous snake." Then Jesus said, "If you, evil as you are, know how to give good things to your children, how much more will your heavenly Father give the Holy Spirit to those who ask Him."

Do you think when we enter our private room and move to the spiritual level of our being in order to be with God, that God is going to hand us over to the devil? Some fundamentalists have the idea that if we empty our minds of thoughts, we open ourselves to the devil. All I can say is, please read the Gospel again. Do you really think that if you open yourself completely to God in trust and love that God will give you a demon?

When we sit in silent prayer, our whole being is begging for the Holy Spirit, the supreme gift of the Father and the Son. There is no greater gift that we can ask for. If we receive the Holy Spirit, we have everything. By entering our private room and closing our eyes to the external and internal environment, we rest in the presence of the Father who loves us and who sent his Son Jesus and his Spirit to lead and guide us to divine union.

To sum up, we don't need to ask for anything at the time of contemplative prayer. At another time, we may be inspired to ask for this or that for someone, or for ourselves. That's fine. But during our private interview with the Divine Therapist, we are praying in secret. We settle into the present moment which is the only place God actually is. God is not in the past and not in the future. God is right now, totally present, totally available. Our best response is to be totally available to that presence. We surrender ourselves after the manner of Mary of Bethany. She gave herself to Jesus, recognizing in him the fullness of the Spirit and the manifestation of the Father's unconditional love.

 FIVE

THE PSYCHOLOGICAL EXPERIENCE OF CENTERING PRAYER

L ET US LOOK at the normal content of the Center-ing Prayer periods. Having assumed a position appropriate for your practice and chosen a symbol of your intention to consent to God's presence, you silently introduce it in your imagination. In the Chris-tian tradition there are two other hallowed ways of expressing in a sacred symbol one's intent to be with God during the time of Centering Prayer. These are the sacred gaze and the sacred breath. The sacred gaze does not make use of visual images. Rather, it is *as if* you were turning inwardly to look at someone you love without imaging anyone or anything partic-ular. You recall that God is embracing you with an infinitely tender gaze, or that you are resting like the

Beloved Disciple on the bosom of Jesus. Likewise, the sacred breath is not a matter of following one's breathing physiologically. It is simply allowing oneself, when thoughts come, to *notice* one's breathing. Both practices are simply expressions of one's intent.

In Centering Prayer, the sacred word, gaze, or breath is sacred not because of its inherent meaning, but because of one's intent, which is to open oneself to God and to the divine action within. Of course, it isn't long before thoughts, feelings, and perceptions start coming down the stream of consciousness. A "thought," in the terminology of Centering Prayer, is any perception whatsoever. It is an umbrella term that includes concepts, memories, plans for the future, feelings, sense perceptions, and reflections.

Whenever attractive or negative thoughts come down the stream of consciousness, we return ever so gently to the sacred symbol we have chosen. The interior dialogue that goes on most of the day and night gradually becomes less intense and absorbing during prayer. The period of prayer becomes a vacation from the false self. Following Jesus' suggestion, we leave outside our awareness all the things that normally preoccupy us. As the movement towards interior silence deepens, there is a sense of pervasive resting, of coming home, of peace. This movement, however, is constantly interrupted by the imagination, which runs in perpetual motion. Since we cannot stop the thoughts, we just put up with them.

Thus there are two levels of awareness. One is the ordinary stream of consciousness with unwanted thoughts going by, and the other is the movement to disregard all thoughts by means of returning again and again to the sacred symbol. In the beginning you may be using the sacred symbol virtually non-stop. But after a few months if you do the practice regularly twice a day for a half an hour or so, you may notice an interesting development. You may become aware, without thinking about it, that you are not interested in the particular thoughts that are passing by.

What is to be done when you are aware of thoughts going by for which you feel no attraction or aversion — in other words, for which you have no interest? Treat them like background music at the supermarket. You have come to buy groceries and the music plays on. Since you can't turn it off, you simply disregard it.

Or again, you may be talking with a friend in an apartment above the street with the windows open. If you are absorbed in the conversation, you may not even notice the noise of the traffic. Then suddenly something happens in the street and sirens start wailing. You feel an urge to go to the window to see what is happening. This is the scenario that occurs when one of our emotional programs for happiness is stimulated by an especially attractive or repulsive thought.

If you get up and go to the window to see what is going on, you are obviously leaving your private room. You just have to return and sit down again. It would be so much easier if, instead of following that interesting thought, you were prompt in realizing that this interruption is not appropriate. In both scenarios, some gesture to renew the conversation is needed. In the case of a conversation between friends, you might just look into the eyes of your companion or you might say, "Excuse me. Where were we?"

The less you do to renew your intention to be with God (hence the brevity of the sacred word), the more easily you forget the interruption and the more continuity you experience in this subtle conversation with God called communing. God's first language is silence. We have to cultivate interior silence to hear the full message.

Let's say you are faithfully reaffirming your original intent to consent to God's presence and action whenever you are thinking other thoughts by returning ever so gently to your sacred symbol. Because of regular practice, your deeply rooted habits of reflecting begin to relax. You notice that you can easily maintain your awareness of God's presence under normal conditions. As a result, you enter quite quickly into a peaceful and restful state that you can maintain with only the occasional use of your sacred symbol.

Some contemplative preparatory practices emphasize attention of the mind, other practices emphasize attention of the heart. The monastic way emphasizes the latter. Purity of heart was the primary objective of the practices of the desert fathers and mothers. They called contemplation "pure prayer," meaning prayer that is coming from a pure intention where the love of God is predominant. They did not seek for any reward such as consolation or enlightenment, or practice for the sake of motives that have their source in the ego, however devout. In point of fact the ego is not devout at all, though it likes to think it is devout and tries to hide behind a variety of religious facades. The spiritual journey is designed to put to rest these facades. But the false self is incredibly clever. Its desires are "worldly." It wants security, affection and esteem, and power and control, as substitutes for waiting upon God in loving attentiveness.

We can change our address, our hairdo, our state of life, our clothes — *anything,* and the false self will not object. But as soon as we try to change *it,* we find ourselves in great conflict. We bring the worldly motivation of the false self into every kind of service, even into prayer. If we once sought to climb the corporate ladder, now in the spiritual life we try to climb the ecclesiastical ladder. But this worldliness is undermined through the development of interior silence. Our ordinary thoughts that reinforce the false self with its desires and aversions are gradually evacuated or laid to rest.

Here we are then, using the sacred symbol to maintain our intention to be with God, when we become aware that we have no interest in the thoughts going by. This is the beginning of the contemplative gifts of the Spirit. God is beginning to answer our basic prayer, "Father, please give me the Holy Spirit." Our will at times is subtly grasped by God. There is a mysterious attraction to interior silence or to the depths of our being. The attraction is like a magnet that draws us into interior silence. At this depth there is a sense that whether we repeat our sacred symbol or not does not matter because we have come to the place where it was meant to guide us. It is like taking a trip to some big city. When you arrive in the city, there is no use buying a ticket to go there.

The sense of God's presence distinguishes this state from mere emptiness or doing nothing. It becomes a state of openness to God that is only occasionally interrupted by an attractive or negative thought passing through. There is no inclination to think of anything, but simply to enjoy the undifferentiated presence of God. At times this presence can become differentiated by a special attraction to the humanity of Jesus or to one of the persons of the Trinity. The spiritual journey is unique to each of us. People have different attractions that help to establish and maintain the growth of interior silence during prayer. The attraction to the center of our being is the awakening to the fact of the divine indwelling. It is not a particular thought, reflection, or feeling, but a sense of being loved or embraced by God. But these experiences are transient and are not the end of the journey. They are ways of orienting us towards what is to come. The Spirit may impart them to some people in great abundance. Others, however, have to live most of the time without them. The main thing everyone can do is the practice. If you do the practice of Centering Prayer regularly, it will do you. There is no substitute for twice a day practice. Talking about it, writing about it, does not do it. Doing it does.

Another level of awareness may open within us after a time. This occurs when the reflective faculties along with the will are more powerfully grasped by God. In this case, God suspends the imagination and memory so they cannot think or reflect. Teresa of Avila reports that in her experience this is quite brief, maybe half an hour at the most. However, one might be in and out of this state in a lengthy period of prayer. A few moments of this grace orientate us powerfully towards divine union. It enormously increases our motivation and determination to pursue this journey. In this state there is no self-reflection. One cannot reflect on the experience until one comes out of it. There is no "I" to enjoy the experience during the time it perdures. If there is self-reflection, this grace is not full union. When we emerge from the experience, there may be the sense of a gap. You may ask, "Was I asleep?" Probably not, unless you were snoring or dreaming. In any case, it is so surprising that you don't know what to make of it. The "butterfly," to put it in the image used by Teresa of Avila, is beginning to emerge from the cocoon. Her image highlights the fact that we do not turn into a butterfly just by wanting to. We have to be willing to weave the cocoon and to stay there in the darkness until in God's appointed time we emerge from it. Then, instead of continuing to crawl through life, we suddenly realize that we can fly.

The practice of Centering Prayer is a good way of responding to God's incredible invitation. The Lord has said, "If anyone loves me, he will keep my words, and the Father will love him and we will come to him and make our abode in him" (John 14:23). Or a further invitation: "I stand at the door and knock. If anyone opens I will come in and have supper with him and he with me" (Rev. 3:20). To paraphrase, "I will identify completely with you and your life situation." This was the meaning of having a meal with others in the Palestinian culture of the time. This is a great development in our prayer, especially when you think of how many times we pray and nothing happens. What counts is to take oneself in hand and devote oneself faithfully to a practice leading to contemplative prayer as well as practices that will bring its effects into daily life. Whoever works at dismantling the false self is a true follower of Christ.

The communication of God, as it gets stronger, is like a sword that goes to the division of soul and spirit. The divine communication requires adequate preparation of the body, mind, and spirit. At some point divine love, for which interior silence is the perfect seedbed, begins to express itself spontaneously in daily life. It perceives God in other people, in events, in nature, in our interior states. It is as though the short interview we had with the Divine Therapist is continued throughout the day.

In short, the Divine Therapist joins us in daily life. He points out, as Jesus did to his disciples, the various aspects of our false self and our mixed motivation. We begin to recognize our attachment to the symbols of security and survival, power and control, affection and esteem in our environment or culture. He points out to us when these are exaggerated, just as he did for Martha. Daily life is where the action is. Prayer, in a sense, is a preparation for action, a perspective from which we can interpret the events of our life as part of the healing process rather than try to manipulate them. Daily life becomes contemplative service, God in us serving God in others. No longer living under the influence or domination of our false selves, we begin to live under the direct influence of the Spirit. We manifest the infinite goodness and tenderness of God.

The whole of life becomes contemplative as a result of the evacuation or dismantling of the obstacles to the action of the Spirit. Whatever prayer practice we started out with has now become, as a result of the infusion of the Seven Gifts of the Spirit, the prayer of the Spirit. As Paul says, "The Spirit intercedes for us with unspeakable groaning" (Rom. 8:26). We do not normally know during prayer what the Spirit is requesting; we simply consent to it.

Our psychological experience or the particular content of prayer is not important. Doing it faithfully with the right intention is. Thus, without going through the stages of exuberant mysticism that Teresa of Avila describes, we can arrive by the hidden ladder of pure faith at the same place. And that place is the transforming union.

Then the permanent awareness of God's presence in a nonjudgmental way accompanies us in all we do. This abiding awareness of God's presence becomes a part of all reality, especially our reality. It adds a fourth dimension to our three-dimensional world.

We watch the action of God within us and around us. We become who we really are at the deepest level, what God is — unconditional love — the total gift of self.

We must not think we are going to experience the liberating process in exactly the same way that John of the Cross did. He had a special ministry that required that his liberation process be hastened. God can put someone through the dark nights in a short time — a few years. For most of us, it is going to take longer.

Now that people live longer, there may be a wonderful flowering of contemplative prayer among senior citizens. Death used to cut short the spiritual journey for a lot of people before they even heard of some of the states described above. In a few years, however, many will be living past a hundred. The last twenty to thirty years of life will provide an enormous potential for contemplative growth. All the stages of the great mystics of past times will be available.

Disciplines for Daily Life

A method of preparing for prayer is like one wing of a bird. If you want to fly, you need the other wing, and that consists of practices for daily life that maintain the alertness to the divine presence that we have discovered in prayer. The spiritual journey is a series of movements into the presence of God at ever-deeper levels. To an established daily practice of contemplative prayer, we need to add appropriate disciplines for daily life. At first, we advise two twenty to thirty minute periods of prayer each day. That is asking a lot of someone living in contemporary society. Questions arise like these: "Where am I going to find the time to spend twenty or thirty minutes every morning and afternoon in prayer? I've got to earn a living, I have a mortgage to pay off, children to bring up and put through school. I can scarcely find an hour to be with my kids each day." The temptation is great to say, "Since I can't enter a monastery, contemplative prayer is not for me." Actually, many people have found that contemplative prayer puts a certain order into their lives. As their minds became clearer and less cluttered, they are better able to choose their priorities. By giving time to contemplative prayer they actually have more time, because they stop doing things that before were useless or unnecessary. John of the Cross has this challenging saying, "If you find that you are working so much that you don't have enough time for your regular time of prayer, just double it!"

There are many traditional practices for daily life. I have suggested a few in two of my books, *Open*

Mind, Open Heart, and, more fully, in *Intimacy With God.* In earlier chapters Lectio Divina was discussed as a means of supporting and nourishing the conceptual background of contemplative prayer.

Another excellent practice is called Guard of the Heart. It is a watchfulness that notices when we lose our sense of peace. We lose peace whenever one of the emotional programs for happiness is frustrated. Then grief, anger, aversion, discouragement, and other afflictive emotions go off. Once afflictive emotions go off, the imagination provides prerecorded tapes that arise of themselves and reenforce the intensity of the emotion. The two are like the wheels of an old clock with interlocking teeth. If one wheel turns, the other has to turn. Accordingly, if you experience a strong emotion, in a second or two you will find yourself with a commentary that is appropriate to it. If someone insults you, before you know it you may find yourself thinking, "How can they do this to me? What can I do to get even?"

Commentaries like these increase the intensity of the original emotion. Soon we find ourselves on an emotional binge that may last a day, a week, and for some people, the rest of their lives. If we learn to let go of afflictive emotions as promptly as they arise, we will enjoy a more durable peace of mind. While Centering Prayer helps us to do that, accompanying practices for daily life help us to do it even more.

Sometimes we may notice a pattern of getting upset in particular circumstances. We can then sleuth back and identify what the particular emotional program for happiness in the unconscious probably is. If you don't have time to go through that process, it may be simpler just to use another practice we call an Active Prayer Sentence. It is like the Jesus prayer, a prayer that you say over and over again until it says itself. John Cassian affirms that the monks of the desert used to sit in their cells weaving baskets saying constantly, "Oh God, come to my assistance. Oh Lord, make haste to help me." Perhaps the more mature monks would just say "Help."

Here is an example of how the Active Prayer Sentence works. Mary Mrozowski was a founder of the Contemplative Outreach spiritual network. During the last year of her life she was noticeably and almost uninterruptedly joyful. That should have been a sign to us that she was ripening for heaven. She died suddenly while giving spiritual counseling. The first time I met Mary, she had driven all the way from Long Island to join our first intensive retreat at Lama, New Mexico. It took her three or four days during which time she said her active prayer sentence nonstop. She continued doing this as a daily practice. One day as she was driving down a road near her home on Long Island, she noticed a youngster on a bicycle ahead of her and at the same time a car coming from behind at a fast clip. The driver, in a hurry and wanting to pass, did not see the bicyclist. He kept honking the horn, meaning, "Get out of the way!" She hesitated to move over lest she hit the youngster. Finally, the man accelerated his car and zoomed around her. Rolling down the window, he yelled obscenities at her and spat right in her face — barely missing her new spring hat. Of course, her emotional programs began to go off, followed at once by a set of prerecorded commentaries: "How can someone do such a thing?" "All men are beasts." Actually, I don't know just what her commentaries were. In any case, as hurt feelings and angry commentaries began to arise, her Active Prayer Sentence rose up along with them and erased them. Into that space the Holy Spirit rushed, saying, "Forgive the guy!" She obeyed and immediately felt as though someone had just given her a bouquet of roses. She drove off down the road in a state of spiritual exultation.

Here is another suggestion. If you have to commute for an hour a day, put a tape deck in your car. In the course of a year you might assimilate more information than if you had completed a graduate program. You could educate yourself, or at the very least, take care of the need for a broad conceptual background for your contemplative practice. And practicing Guard of the Heart at the same time would take care of your emotional frustrations.

In addition, a retreat once a year would deepen your daily practice, especially if the retreat is long enough, like five or preferably eight full days. If that is not possible because of your situation and responsibilities, take a retreat day once a month, preferably along with others doing the same kind of prayer practice. The support of similarly minded people helps to persevere in prayer in difficult times.

In any case, whatever effort you put into remaining in God's presence in everyday life will favorably affect your prayer and help you to advance in interior silence. The movement into interior silence tends to transmute all your activities into contemplative service.

SIX

QUESTIONS
AND ANSWERS

Q. I feel strongly drawn to the Father in Centering Prayer. I also feel a void in my relationship with Jesus as a Roman Catholic. I know about him but I don't feel that I am close to him. This void concerns me. Can you say something about this?

A. When you are practicing a nonconceptual form of prayer habitually, your ordinary way of relating to Jesus may change. The conversational aspect during the time of formal prayer gives way to a mysterious attraction for silence. Silence is more characteristic of the presence of the one whom in Christianity we call the Father. The Father is the source of infinite possibilities. The Son is the expression of all that the Father is. The Son returns everything that he has received to the Father, utterly empties himself, and becomes nothing, so to speak. The experience of a kind of void in our conceptual understanding of Christ can be misinterpreted as a loss of devotion to Jesus or the disregard of his sacred humanity. Teresa of Avila was very concerned about the danger of losing contact with the sacred humanity of Jesus.

In actual fact, what may be happening is that we are becoming identified with Jesus. We have entered into a new kind of relationship that is not so much one-on-one, as one inside the other. In actual fact it is an increase of Jesus' presence that gives rise to this sense of inner void that we are dealing with. Christ is now praying in us. We don't separate ourselves from him as we did when he was a presence outside of us. We become, so to speak, the Word of God. We don't normally think about something that we already are. We take it for granted. Our psychological state may be a void with regard to Jesus, but the reality of our experience is that our union with him has reached a certain level where we no longer think of him as separate from us or we from him.

Q. You mentioned Satan. Is he an actual spirit or being who has power over humanity?

A. The problem of evil and Satan is a very complicated question. The Christian tradition, as other religious traditions, has always believed in demons and Satan, the latter as kind of boss of the evil spirits. Scripture tells us in several places that Jesus spoke of Satan. For example, "I saw Satan like lightning falling from heaven" (Luke 10:18).

The Tibetan Buddhists have an intriguing description of how evil fits into the spiritual journey. In their view, the demons are personifications of the dark side of our unconscious, and consequently, there is a certain period in the spiritual life in which, for all practical purposes, they are real. In actual fact, however, according to this teaching, they are simply a stage of spiritual development. Similarly, there are angels who are personifications of the positive side of our unconscious. As one rises from stage to stage towards higher states of consciousness, both angels and demons disappear and the soul is reunited with ultimate reality.

While I think that a lot of things that used to be attributed to demons are simply manifestations of the false self, I believe that demons do exist. I have met people who had experiences of demons. For instance, a young monk came to me once in the middle of the night. He was terrified and said, "I was lying in bed and something got on top of my chest and nearly suffocated me. I knew it was the demon." Usually our intuitive faculties can sense when evil is around, just as we sometimes feel when there is a certain evil energy in a room or in people. Then the monk said, "The devil started pulling me out of bed."

If this is a projection of the unconscious, it's pretty powerful stuff!

There are cases in history such as exorcisms where a possessed person reportedly had the strength of three or four strong men. In the Acts of the Apostles there is a passage where a demon mocks seven itinerant exorcists, saying, "Jesus I recognize and Paul I know, but who are you?" (cf. Acts 19:13–16). Whereupon the possessed man proceeded to send them packing. In addition, there are some acts of human maliciousness that are beyond belief. Think of the horrors of this century such as the Holocaust, Cambodia, the Russian Gulag, Armenia, Rwanda, Bosnia, and Kosovo. Is this just the human condition or does the demon reinforce human malice? Do extreme forms of malice point to a demonic element? Scott Peck wrote a book called *The People of the Lie*. In it he writes that he did not believe in demons until he attended an exorcism. That changed his mind. So if you are in doubt about the existence of demons, you might do the same.

One last point is extremely important. We believe as Christians that Jesus, through his passion, death, and resurrection, has completely taken away the devil's power. The only way the devil can have any influence over us is if we deliberately invite his help. There are large numbers of satanic cults in this country. The damage that is done to participants and sometimes to innocent people is appalling. For one thing, it is very difficult to get out of such cults. Stay away from any kind of satanic rituals, pacts, or persons who are involved in such practices.

Q. When persons are meditating and they feel overwhelmed with a compulsive thought, evil impulse, or some experience of evil, what would you suggest that they do?

A. The first thing I would suggest is that they return to their sacred symbol. Sometimes primitive emotions are so strong that the sacred symbol or a mantra is not a help. We feel submerged in a sea of distress. In that case, let the pain of the unwanted and compulsive temptation become your sacred symbol of consenting to God's presence and action within you. Wait out the storm with trust in God's mercy and power, remembering that God is present even in the greatest of storms. If the situation continues, they might consider consulting a psychotherapist to rule out psychological factors that might be present We should not assume too easily that demons are involved in our lives even when we believe that it can happen.

Q. Does the Spirit come to those who meditate in a non-Christian contemplative form such as Vipassana and Buddhist meditation? And when a Christian meditates in the Vipassana form, is she or he still open to the Holy Spirit?

A. Definitely. It is important for Roman Catholics to be fully aware that the Second Vatican Council in its teaching on the non-Christian religions made a hundred eighty degree turn from the previous teaching and explicitly recognized that the Holy Spirit is at work in them. The church now holds what is theologically called "an inclusive position"; that is to say, persons practicing other religions reach salvation in virtue of Jesus' passion, death, and resurrection, even if they are not aware of who he is. As Christians, we believe that Jesus is the savior of the human family and that through his divine nature he has been present to every human being from the beginning of time. In other words, all people are called to be saved through God's infinite mercy, whether they know the historical Jesus or not.

There are many people who know Christianity only in a very distorted form, and could not possibly identify with the kind of religion that they see expressed in the lives of some Christians. Obviously, it is not Christ they are rejecting, but a distorted manifestation of the Christian religion.

Religion is not the only means of coming to know God. Nature, spiritual friendship, conjugal love, service of others, art — these are all ways in which God calls people to himself. Religion is only one way. There may be personal reasons why one cannot identify with any religion at all. God takes all that into account and provides other paths. Moreover, like the spokes of a wheel, all paths to God tend to come closer to each other as they come closer to God, who is the center and source of them all. For example, it is normal for someone who has taken the religious path to begin to perceive the wonders of God in nature as a further means of uniting with God.

Q. What is the connection between contemplative prayer and world problems like war, pestilence, sexism, and racism?

A. Contemplative prayer is a major contribution to the diminishing of world problems of injustice, prejudice, health, and peace. If enough people progressed in contemplative prayer, they could reduce a sizable portion of the negativity in our world. The atmosphere of the planet has been filled with negativity from the endless procession of false selves that have peopled it from the beginning of time, including ourselves. But charity (divine love) is so strong that just a little of it can negate an enormous amount of negativity. A critical number of people actually meditating is an insight our Hindu and Buddhist friends also have. Contemplative prayer enables people to clean up their lives through the insights of self-knowledge that flow from such a practice, so that at least they don't continue to pour negative energy into the atmosphere. We would all do everyone on earth a great favor if we would die to our false selves and pour the divine energy of pure love into the atmosphere instead of the energy of our selfish drives for happiness. When contemplative persons get together in prayer, there is an enormous amount of positive energy generated, especially if they have been practicing a long time.

Q. How can enlightenment come without purification? I thought the two went hand in hand. Can you have one without the other?

A. I don't think you can have enlightenment without purification, certainly not full enlightenment. In Eastern religions, there are different stages of development such as I described in talking about the household of Bethany. Thus, there are levels of samadhi in Hinduism and Buddhism that are recognized as stages of enlightenment. There was a study by an American psychologist who visited a number of enlightened teachers in Thailand.[1] He found only one who was fully enlightened. One Zen master told me he knew very few Zen masters whom he regarded

---

1. Jack Engler in *Transformations of Consciousness: Conventional and Contemplative Perspectives on Development* (Boston: Shambhala, 1996).

as fully enlightened. Thus, we are talking about partial enlightenment. If so, the false self is still in some degree active.

As we saw in discussing Lazarus as a paradigm of Christian enlightenment, the only cure for the false self is death. Without the Night of Spirit or its equivalent, no one is fully enlightened. Without that profound purification, one can make mistakes and lead people astray. In the Christian scheme of things, Jesus alone is fully enlightened. In his glorified body he is in us and we are in him, closer to us than any teacher, because through his Spirit he dwells within us. Everyone else who teaches in the Christian tradition is simply a disciple of Jesus.

Q. What is infused contemplation?

A. This is a term that John of the Cross has hallowed. In general, it means that the Seven Gifts of the Spirit, in particular the contemplative gifts of wisdom, knowledge, and understanding, have taken over one's prayer. You no longer have need of any method because the Spirit prays in you. Teresa of Avila, in *The Interior Castle,* describes the grace of interior recollection that is the infused sense of God's presence; next, the prayer of quiet in which God grasps the will while the other faculties wander about; partial union in which the faculties of imagination and memory are suspended temporarily; and finally, full union in which there is no self-reflection.

There are thus levels or stages of infused contemplation. The levels I have just mentioned do not include the Night of Spirit and the Transforming Union. It is only in the Transforming Union that the awareness of union with God is permanent and never goes away. Bridal mysticism, however, is not the end of the journey. Beyond that are the stages of contemplation that are described by the great women mystics of the late Middle Ages like Hadewijch of Brabant, Mechtild of Magdeburg, and Marguerite Porete.

Centering Prayer is a bridge between discursive meditation and our efforts to develop the receptive attitude suitable for infused contemplation. There is a kind of no man's land, so to speak, between our gentle efforts to be still before God in prayer and the Holy Spirit approaching us with the gift of infused contemplation. In this middle space, we do not know for certain whether the Spirit is predominant or our very gentle efforts. Infused contemplation, at least in the Carmelite tradition, is the habitual state of waiting upon God in loving attentiveness. John of the Cross describes infused contemplation as "totally receptive." Once in a while serious troubles come up, and then you may need to slip back into your former method to support you.

Q. *The next question concerns tears during the time of meditation. Are tears always emotional baggage or is there a spiritual value to these tears?*

A. Tears are a great gift. There is even a prayer in *The Roman Sacramentary* for the "gift of tears." The fathers and mothers of the Desert regarded them as a great treasure. Tears soften up the heart and open it to God in a wonderful way that no amount of reflecting can do. Tears are normally a sign of grief or compunction. They can also be a sign of a joy that is so great that there is no way to express it except to allow the tears to flow.

There is also a third source of tears that is significant in the process of the liberation of the unconscious. Most of us in this culture, especially men, have suppressed grief. Tears may be the first sign of the unloading of the unconscious. It often happens in Centering Prayer intensive retreats in which the participants pray four or five hours a day. They may experience so much physical and spiritual rest that the body too rests more profoundly than ever before. As a result, one's emotional defenses go down, and the first thing that usually comes to consciousness is the repressed grief of a lifetime. Tears may pour down one's cheeks for the entire time of prayer without one's knowing the cause. Actually, the body through deep rest has gotten permission to unload grief that has been stored in the organism and hindering the free flow of the natural energies and grace. If you get into sobbing, then for the sake of others in the prayer group, I would suggest going outside and doing your crying in a private place. But don't suppress it. It is liberating and healthy.

Q. How do you define sin?

A. Jesus has taken upon himself the sins of the world. He became *flesh*, that is, he became a member of the human race precisely as fallen. This is the human condition that I described above as the emotional programs for happiness and overidentification with one's primary group. The human condition involves the tendency to sin, described in theology as the "capital sins," a doctrine developed by Evagrius of Pontus in the fourth century. The tendency to sin is rooted in the energy centers that we create as infants and toddlers to deal with survival and security, affection and esteem, and power and control issues.

These needs become drives or demands to experience happiness in ways in which we are more or less driven to seek it. Of course, there is no hope of finding it. As infants we don't know what true happiness is. Nor can we make moral judgments that are really free until about thirteen or fourteen, and perhaps even later in our culture. When we reach the age of reason and free choice, we normally ratify our exaggerated demands for security and survival, affection and esteem, and power and control. We then tend to trample on the rights and needs of others and our own true good. And *that* is personal sin. For a morally free act there has to be full knowledge of the seriousness of the evil involved and full consent of the will. We thought sin was fairly easy to commit in centuries past but now, with our greater awareness of psychological factors, we may wonder how many people are sufficiently free to commit serious sin or to make lifelong commitments.

Q. What should one do when compulsive thoughts keep coming into one's meditation time?

A. The question arises, "Why are compulsive thoughts coming at this time?" One reason may be that one may suffer from the affliction of scruples. Another is that one may have an addiction of some kind. We naturally tend to think of our addictions when the mind is not occupied with particular considerations or images. When they become overwhelming, we carry them out in active life. Hence, it is no wonder we think about them during prayer. If it is only an occasional problem, I would simply do what you do with any thought that comes down the stream of consciousness during nondiscursive meditation. If you are following the teaching of John Main, keep saying the mantra. If you are in Centering Prayer, return to the sacred symbol you have chosen.

Scruples are one of the greatest afflictions in life. Such persons love God very much, but they can't move hand or foot without the fear of doing something wrong. They get no enjoyment out of their service of God. It is a very difficult problem to treat because it is involved with emotionally charged thoughts from early childhood that are deeply embedded. That is why the way that religion is taught to children needs a great deal of careful thought and should not be put into the hands of somebody who simply picks up a catechism. It would almost be better not to teach a child religion than to do it improperly. The fear of God should not be instilled into little children. In actual fact it is a technical term in Scripture meaning a right relationship with God. And that relationship is trust. Gratitude and trust are the basis of a healthy relationship with God.

Psychological dynamics may be responsible for compulsive thoughts in a particular case. It is better to have a friendly attitude towards whatever one's compulsions may be. As Thérèse of Lisieux put it, "No matter how wild my thoughts, I accept them all for the love of God." No thought or desire can harm us unless we consent. Our thoughts are like clouds in the sky. They come and they go. To develop the habit of letting go of every afflictive thought or emotion as soon as it arises is the best ascesis during prayer. Avoid thinking about anything that bothers you during prayer. Let God act. If you are worried about your faults, you will never overcome them. Simply take them as they come. Watch them before, watch them happening, watch them afterwards. Let God work with your faults without being overanxious about them. Our efforts will never accomplish the necessary healing. Only God's grace can do that. To cooperate with the Divine Therapist is work enough. Since God is infinitely merciful and wishes to transform us into Godself, what is there to be worried about? God has the situation in hand. Sometimes our efforts do more harm than good and make things worse. There is a delicate balance between accepting the pain of the disturbing thought, situation, or emotion, and not making too much of it. It is like water off a duck's back. Yes, you are going to get wet, but let the water roll off you. God is sometimes playing with us; sometimes a little roughly, but always lovingly.

Q. I have been meditating for many years, yet I have no spiritual experience. Can you address that?

A. Many people meditate because they receive consolation once in a while. Every now and then they get a ray of light or a sense of peace that supports them on the journey. But someone who is not receiving consolations and still perseveres deserves the first prize. John of the Cross is a great help here. One of his major contributions to the knowledge of the spiritual journey is the alternative he describes for the exuberant mysticism of Teresa of Avila. He teaches that there is also a mysticism of pure faith, which he calls the "hidden ladder," which is characterized by darkness and habitual dryness all the way to transforming union. The ladder of pure faith is like taking the back stairs of Teresa's *Interior Castle*. But what difference does it make when you are trying to get to the top of the castle whether you take the main staircase with its gilded banisters or the back stairs assigned to the servants? The main thing is to reach the top. In John of the Cross's view, the Night of Sense does not necessarily lead, as Teresa seems to think, to the exuberant mysticism of the prayer of quiet union and full union. Some and perhaps even most persons who are led into the Night of Sense continue in it until it turns into the Night of Spirit, without a period of profound spiritual consolation.

Ruth Burrows in her book *Guidelines for Mystical Prayer* distinguishes between "lights on" spirituality and a "lights off" spirituality. According to her, both ways lead to the transforming union. Those who go the path of exuberant mysticism (lights on) run the risk of becoming attached to their spiritual experiences. The way of pure faith or the hidden ladder —

John of the Cross's contribution to the mystical journey — is a great consolation to people who have spent years on the journey and felt that they got nowhere because they had no consolation. My answer to the question is, "You are very close to the top, just keep going."

Q. I am a Zen Buddhist and I have been taught not to expect to gain anything, including peace of mind, from Zen. Can one hope to gain happiness or relief from suffering through Centering Prayer?

A. There is no spiritual practice that I know of that is guaranteed to bring complete relief from suffering. A Zen master, Joshu Roshi Sasaki, came to the Spencer Abbey for seshin once or twice a year for ten years while I was the abbot there. If I understood him correctly, his students are not encouraged to expect anything in Zen practice for substantially the same reasons that I gave when talking about the divine indwelling. We already have all that we possibly need. We just need to believe it.

Zen, if I understand it correctly, teaches that you must not desire enlightenment because you have already got it. The questioner might consult authorities in the Zen Buddhist world to see whether or not to desire anything for ourselves is a hindrance to getting it. The desire itself indicates that we are attached to some project of the false self. Both the path to the

transforming union and the path to Buddhist enlightenment teach the opposite. They come to us by not
seeking self in any form, including stages of enlightenment or divine union. No doubt, it is hard not to
hope for some reward for all our efforts, but it is
a sign of progress when we move from the hope of
reward to simply accepting God as God is and all
reality as it is, without seeking or reflecting on ourselves. As soon as we reflect on ourselves, we are
back in our own private universe with the false self
at the center. That is not the true universe.

*Q. Is personal suffering redemptive and how is
that so, if it is so?*

A. Personal suffering is certainly redemptive of
ourselves and at the same time of everybody else.
This is the divine plan, at least in the Christian
scheme of things. Jesus has become a human being
and taken on the human condition — that is, sinfulness and sin — taking all the consequences of them
into himself. Jesus' descent into hell is the symbol
of this psychological and spiritual impoverishment.
Notice, the descent into hell is a phrase that appears
in the Apostles creed. Hell is not a geographical loca-
tion. Rather, Jesus is believed to have descended into
the psychological state of hell and undergone the ultimate alienation from God that is the essence of sin.
In other words, "he who did not know sin, was made

to be sin" (2 Cor. 5:21), as Paul teaches. He who is in the bosom of the Father accepted, for love of us and our redemption, total alienation from the Father. Jesus, in his passion, death, and descent into hell, threw away the sense of his personal union with the Father. Christ's sacrifice of himself for us, therefore, is not only his death on the cross, but the psychological, spiritual, and personal alienation from the infinite Good which only he could have fully known as God's consubstantial Son. It is from that depth of his humility from having taken the lowest place, that he is able to heal everyone else who is alienated from God and to restore everyone to innocence, freedom, and union with God. That is the meaning of his resurrection, and that is what the full extent of redemption really means.

God goes a step further. God loves us so much that he wants us to participate in the redemption of the human family.

When our sufferings are joined to Christ's, they become redemptive for us personally. Then our sufferings become redemptive for those we love and others whom we may never know — for those in the past who needed help and those in the future who may need help. There is no time or space in the redemptive perspective. Everything is now. Eternal values cut through chronological time at every moment. If we accept our own redemption, we have entered into the Paschal Mystery. This is the ultimate purpose of the contemplative life. We become what the Buddhists call a bodhisattva, which is someone who is enlightened but who declines to go into final enlightenment until everybody else enters first. This marvelous concept is very close in its inspiration (though maybe not in its explanation) to the Christian idea of Jesus suffering for each human being from the beginning of time until the end. Christ's suffering was not limited to the torments that the authorities inflicted on him; his chief suffering was our sinfulness and the consequences. When we feel alienated from God, we are very close to Christ, because now we know how he felt in his isolation. The great project that the Father entrusted to Jesus is the salvation of every human being. This is "the mystery hidden from eternity in God" (Eph. 3:9) in which we are invited to participate.

SEVEN

A LOOK AT
THE FUTURE

WHAT can the Christian contemplative tradition offer to the world in the coming millennium? What might be the major elements of a spiritual life rooted in the Christian tradition and at the same time in dialogue with the other world religions, modern science, and the healing arts?

The great gift that contemplative persons offer is the experience of the divine presence. Who is going to bring this realization into society if not those who are experiencing it?

To be in dialogue with the other world religions requires the contemplative experience because all in their fully developed spiritual disciplines have experienced it. This fact suggests that the members of the other world religions must henceforth be fully accepted as brothers and sisters, greatly loved by

God and blessed with resources of immense value to contribute to us and to the world at large.

What is called for is the collaboration of all those who share true human values, especially among those religions that have been entrusted with long traditions of spiritual experience. This is the great treasure of humanity that now needs to be shared. From this perspective, one may rightly ask whether in the next millennium the purpose of the Christian religion is to make converts as we have been instructed up till now. In virtue of the development of global consciousness, a new understanding of the Gospel is required. God is the Father of all men and women. Perhaps the first duty of the Christian religion now is not so much to propagate itself as to foster communion with the other world religions.

This communion would mean that for the first time in history, Christians would manifest by their behavior and attitudes that all the members of the human family are children of God, that each religion has its part to play in revealing the true God, and above all, that God wants the diverse religions of the world to live together in peace.

Unfortunately, up till now the religions of the world have been one of the chief sources of violence. Given the human condition, the greatest security that people have is their own particular religion. Hence any threat to it is a threat to their personal security system. We tend to be overprotective of our particular religious persuasion not so much out of religious conviction, but because we need to enjoy the security of enjoying God's special favor and to feel better than other people. This is not religion. It is rather an expression of the false self.

It is only through genuine contemplative experience that these naive loyalties are laid to rest so that we can see one another as the beloved child of the Father and as persons for whom Christ has died.

The modern sciences are friends too. In recent generations religion and science have often been at each other's throats. Actually science is a friend. In the next century it will be important to have an ongoing and in-depth dialogue with science. The cutting edge of physics is the search for the unknown. Science, as Einstein put it, is basically a spiritual search to find out God's thoughts.

This brings us to the subject of the healing arts. Up till the end of this century, Christian theology has been discussed in terms of Neo-Platonism or Aristotelianism. Now we have to leave behind our former ways of trying to explain the Christian mystery and open ourselves to the great Hebrew intuition that the human being is a body-mind-spirit composite.

What might be the impact of the contemplative dimension of the Gospel on the various Christian denominations, contemporary society, and the global consciousness that seems to be emerging? At this conference the Christian denominations represented here have manifested the capacity to bond beyond denominational boundaries. Here in daily prayer and meditation we have opened to the living Christ and to the experience of the Spirit. Surely this is what our respective doctrinal persuasions are designed to bring about. In this assembly we have witnessed a paradigm of what unity among the varieties of Christian community can be or really is. Unity cannot be found in agreement in the details of doctrine. It can only be found in the lived experience of Christ that we have been tasting. The contemplative dimensions of the Gospel, cultivated by all the denominations, is the only way the unity, for which Christ prayed and died, will ever happen.

This will require significant shifts in our mindsets. Most of us have what we might call a religious superego — that is to say, the way we think (or have been brought up to think) dictates religious practice. In Northern Ireland this has led to shooting one another. In Rwanda, eighty percent of the people engaged in the massacres were Christians and most of these were Roman Catholics. What does that say about missionary work? The massacres proved that tribal blood is stronger than baptismal water. Certain missionary congregations are rethinking their ministry as missionaries in the light of what happened there. The preaching of the Gospel was just never heard.

One of the great visions that has emerged in our time — a new way of looking at missionary work and the relationship between the world religions — is the extraordinary witness of the seven Trappist martyrs of Algeria who were put to death by Muslim extremists. I mention them because they manifest a new kind of evangelization. It is the dialogue of presence even unto death. The monks lived among the impoverished Muslims around the monastery and shared with them their agricultural know-how, studied the Koran with them, offered them hospitality, and gave them help in whatever way they could. From the perspective of the Islamic extremists, that was their crime. The Koran says that if a holy man from another religion lives in solitude, no one can touch him. On the other hand, if he lives with the local people and reaches out to them, he loses his protected status and can be treated like other unwanted foreigners. Some of the monks' friends had been killed. They knew the dangers and had the choice to leave at any time. They held extensive dialogues among themselves to discern whether they should stay or leave. They opted to remain.

Their decision captures the essence of Christ's message which is to be present to people not just with words, but with one's whole being, ready to lay down one's life for one's friends and neighbors if that should be God's will. They did not desire martyrdom because they did not want to lay a guilt trip on anybody. They just wanted to live daily life in communion with their impoverished neighbors and to improve the quality of their own lives. They reflected on the two thieves on each side of Jesus on the cross and realized that they could be either one of those thieves. In light of that insight, they prayed for the oppressors as well as for the oppressed. They prayed not only for those who were being killed in that tragic situation but for the killers as well. And they prayed that if they themselves should be killed, their killers would be forgiven because of their good intention according to their lights. For them what mattered was to be totally at God's disposal, whatever this might mean, and to live in the present moment as best they could as witnesses to God's infinite tenderness for the Muslims around them.

Their letters have been circulated in France and read like a manual of nonviolence. The Fruits of the Spirit and the Beatitudes were at work in them, but at work in the simplest kind of way. They were not trying to make a splash, they just wanted to improve their daily lives by greater hospitality, smiling at the people they did not like, and putting up with people who interrupted their solitude. They wanted to be ordinary people with extraordinary love. Their witness will appear more strongly in the next century. How we live our ordinary lives reveals the face of Christ more than proselytizing. It is in fostering communion with our neighbors whatever their religion that the true face of Christ emerges.

These martyrs did not accept the concept of having enemies. For them the basic human vocation is to be a brother or sister. In the parable of the Prodigal Son where both sons acted outrageously, the Father did not ask either of them to do penance. He just asked them to live together in peace. That was all. That message, the heart of the Gospel, has to be communicated by who we are and how we live.

Contemplative practices are totally in the service of that project. What the Christian religion might contribute to global spirituality is the personal love of the Father in Jesus Christ for every human being. To love one another as Christ has loved us is the goal of Christianity. Christ is the enlightened one. It is to him that all our practices and rituals are pointing.

What form might a Christian contemplative contribution take to the emerging spiritual consciousness in the coming millennium? It seems to me that one major contribution is to form new types of communities that support communion in contemplative prayer and in finding new expressions of it. The love of God is so powerful that no one can just sit on it. It is bound to express itself. We have to think not just of praying together but how we can reach out and support each other in helping those in prison, the homeless, the hungry, the oppressed, everyone in need. Above all, direct attention to the most unbearable problem in the world today, which is the destitution of the poor. Jesus said: "The poor you will always have with you." But destitution is something else. That is our responsibility. It is not God's will. Whatever the benefits of the market economy, if it does not do something about the one-sidedness of the global economy, it will not last. It will simply disintegrate like all other forms of government that are not inspired by the values of the Gospel or at least by good human values.

The Spirit may be asking the Christian denominations to join forces with each other and with the other world religions in addressing human needs and social issues. The God in us is calling us to serve the God in others.